THE PLANNER

ESSENTIAL TACTICS TO BEING

happy & SUCCESSFUL

PHYLENCIA TAYLOR

BEAUTY CULTURALIST

THE CAUSE CULTURE
THECAUSECULTURE.ORG

50% of All Proceeds Go to The CauseCulture.Org
Conventional and Unconventional Scholarships

ACKNOWLEDGEMENTS

FOR

Chance, My Amazing Evolving Boy.

TO

Those who believe in themselves enough to Try and Do.

DEDICATED TO

All the brave women that came before us.

Women that have suffered, sacrificed, supported,

held another sister up, stood-up, fought for,

made a come-back and loved hard–

so that we can choose our journey today.

Thank you.

In Honor of Women's History Month.

CONTENTS

BUSINESS

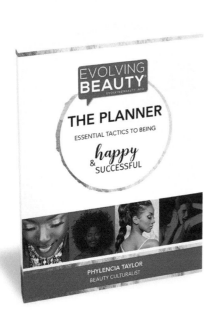

LIFE

EVOLVING**BEAUTY**®

Cultivated Tools to Boost the Evolution to Success
@EVOLVINGBEAUTY.INFO | #BOOSTEVOLUTION

BARNES & NOBLE   amazon

© EvolvingBeaty.Info   + Other Fine Retailers

1.0 INTRODUCTION

POET AND AWARD-WINNING Author, Maya Angelo said,

"My mission in life is not merely to survive, but to thrive; and to do so with some passion, some compassion, some humor, and some style."

To thrive in business equals success. But to thrive in business and your personal life, that equates to being Happy & Successful.

My goal in creating Evolving Beauty, THE PLANNER is to share real-life Evolving Beauties stories of women in the beauty industry. Thriving women, WOMEN IN MOTION, Significant because they inspire. Uniquely important for first-generation female entrepreneurs and executives. Women navigating the unknown. Women without the privilege of childhood business model memories, business family friends or business related holiday perks. Their plight to thrive and not just survive has an entirely different meaning. It requires enhanced goals, planning and discipline. A paradigm shift in mindset, a robust persistence, and belief in self.

The intention of THE PLANNER is two-fold: first, to Inspire. To share the journeys of real-life, real-time business women who surrendered they life they had, to create the life they wanted. Women working to embody the perfect combination - the balance of being Happy & Successful!

The second tool is a Powerful Patterned Framework Tool; has two tools that support Self & Brand Mastery: first, The 4-Step Brand Mastery Worksheet. Business success aligned with being happy. The second tool is a Powerful Patterned Framework Tool; it defines annual goals and priorities with monthly and daily positive patterns to propel the evolution for success. Small daily tactical steps that over time becomes big, goal smashing successes. The evolving journey to being Happy & Successful. THANK YOU for purchasing Evolving Beauty, *Essential Insider Tactics to being Happy & Successful.

As a Culturalist and Beauty Marketing Executive, I study the beliefs, culture, and behavior of people, primarily women. Even before I won a local beauty pageant as a teenager, in my hometown of upstate, NY. I understood that beauty can shape a woman's identity and the world around her.

After working with Fortune 500 companies and C-Suite Executives for a decade, I discovered powerful insights about what women in business.

Throughout my career as an Executive at companies like Wella Corporation, Johnson Products, Carol's Daughter, Blue Flame, Fortune Brands and LVMH Wine & Spirits to name a few, I've spent countless hours providing professional support for past employers and former/current clients. While backstage, in board rooms, conference rooms, production rooms, green rooms and VIP rooms, you begin to gain valuable insight about people patterns. The patterns of successful people, the happy and not-so-happy.

There was a time in my career when I just wasn't happy. I worked 50-70 hours a week; I wasn't in a relationship, and I didn't have a family of my own. I was just unhappy, I thought, "Why am I doing this again?" I soon realized not only was I unhappy; but I also looked at those I spent the most time with, the executives around were unhappy too.

I yearned for change, and my journey made a pivot to create more value, more substance, more Happy & Successful--personally and professionally. I learned to quickly distinguish between happy and unhappy people; I began to study their patterns. I've met hundreds of successful people, but few were genuinely happy.

I'm proud of the professional work I've done as a former employee, consultant, peer, colleague and at times, a friend. I'm equally as proud of the healing and work I've done to get closer to Happy & Successful. As a personal development enthusiast, I've spent thousands of dollars on books, seminars and workshops, including completing personal development course, Personal Dynamics Leadership. (Similar to the world-renowned Landmark coursework)

I designed THE PLANNER from a culmination of courses, insights, and experiences. A framework to develop patterns and useful essential tools and tactics to thrive, to become Happy & Successful.

As a single mother, consultant, entrepreneur, educator and social servant, my life is no easy task, with or without a loving tribe. I teach communication courses at an Atlanta University, and have a M.A. in Strategic Communication. However, I don't profess to be the Happiest or the most Successful. I am passionate about the cultivation and evolution of women, being better--Happy & Successful!

I am a Woman in Motion.

A Woman in Beauty.

I trust MY journey to be

Happy & Successful. So should you.

At Evolving Beauty®, our philosophy lives and breathes in trusting the journey. When we accept that seasons, situations and relationships change and that change is good, it allows us to resist less, to breathe with full breathes, and less stress. One of the ways as humans, as women, we express our higher selves is through growth. If we aren't evolving and growing, we're simply existing.

You've selected THE PLANNER to support your evolution; you want your life to look differently, better next year than it does today. And so do we at Evolving Beauty. The growth from where and who you are now, to where and who you wish to become. I want this planner to be used as a tool to help execute your biggest dreams. #BoostTheEvolution.

As a woman, especially a one of color, to do, create or build anything outside of the "status quo" requires a strong sense of self, a thick skin, and a healthy, loving tribe. A robust network and support system. Being prepared is vital, but instituting advanced strategies with long-term alternatives (Plan B) is paramount.

The further planning, the more prepared to overcome and persist through the inevitable "no's."

I've talked with hundreds of women on the book tour for my debut book, Evolving Beauty, the Business of Beauty in a New Age. Engaged with countless women regarding the popular e-worksheet, "Brand Mastery." Here are some of the findings uncovered from that communication.

The Planner has two powerful tactics to support the findings.

1. The 4-Step Brand Mastery Worksheet

    and

2. The Framework Tools are the tactics provided in THE PLANNER to identify, prioritize and implement positive patterns for your success.

LOVE & SUPPORT

99% of women said having a healthy relationship is important to them. Women want the love of a relationship coupled with the love of family and friends. A loving, healthy tribe cements a greater purpose to the passion, a woman's pursuit.

THE VALUE OF TIME

Time, it is arguably the most honest commodity of life. It plays fair, whereas everyone gets the same amount, every day. Time gives no privilege to upbringing, environment, class, ethnicity, education, title, stature, position or credentials. Therefore, where and with whom we spend our time, is vital to our evolution, our journey.

FIND YOUR TRIBE

98% of women said having a circle of women as friends are important to them. The support of other women who understand us is critical to our journey.

(Research provided by Shine Beauty Culture Consultancy.)

Beauty industry peers or women from different backgrounds. Nonetheless, someone to lend an ear or a hug or advice to soothe or boost the evolution.

NETWORKING/ MENTORING

Women, especially first generation entrepreneurs, need the leverage and support of one another. When like-minded people, pursuing like-minded goals come together, the opportunities are boundless, and success, limitless.

The demands of today's aspirational, goal oriented women are robust. Stronger than ever. The requirements of creating a business, as a beauty intrepreneur or entrepreneur, can feel completely unbalanced and overwhelming. Our cups runneth over.

THE PLANNER, released in the month of March, Women's History Month, in honor of all the Women in Motion that came before to us so to provide greater FREEDOMS, that we may choose our journey.

2.0 WOMEN IN MOTION

DEAR EVOLVING BEAUTIES,

My deepest thank-you to the hundreds of women I spoke with while on the Evolving Beauty debut book tour and the countless social media messages from the "Brand Mastery" e-worksheet, the inspiration for this planner.

A special thank-you to the Women in Motion. Twelve (12) Beauty Executives, Founders, Bloggers/Vloggers and Beauty Professionals that shared their journeys, wisdom, passion, and pain points in THE PLANNER.

Thank you for sharing, trusting the evolving journey--to Being Happy & Successful.

Your journey will inspire other women. May you always evolve.

Love & Light,

-PT

XII WOMEN IN MOTION •

ROCHELLE GRAHAM
THE BEAUTY EMPRESS
@AlikayNaturals
"Always be true to yourself, Remember who you are and where you've from."

TANESHA BARNES
BEAUTY'S FREEDOM FIGHTER
@TBarnesBeauty
"When you see the beauty in yourself, you walk the earth differently."
T. Barnes

TIFFINI GATLIN
AN EVOLVING INNOVATOR
@LatchednHooked
"Mistakes and Failures are Preparation for Greater Opportunities"
LATCHED HOOKED

DESHAWN HATCHER
MASTER MAKEUP ARTIST
@DeShawnHatcher
"There's Only ONE YOU, Live Your Life!"

CARLINE DARGENSON
THE HAIR ARTIST
@InStylHairCare
"Business is Never Personal"
INSTIL

RACHEL ODEM
THE TRIPLE THREAT OF BEAUTY INFLUENCERS
@RachelOBeauty
"You can do anything you put your mind to, and work for."

ERICA DOUGLAS
BEAUTY PIONEER
@SisterScientist
"A WOMAN who does not require validation, is the most feared on the planet"

DANA HILL
THE NATURAL GIFTER
@Cocotique
"Success is not the Key to Happiness, Happiness is the Key to Success"
COCOTIQUE

SOPHIA WHITE
THE NAIL ARTIST
@SophieInHarlem
"Have the Courage to Have Courage"
sophia!

JAE NASH
THE VOICE OF INSPIRATION
@GirlPowerHour
"Keep Your Head In the Game & Surround Yourself with Positive People"
POWER

TANYA GALLAGHER
THE LOVE PENCHER
@PenchantBare
"Of Course You Can"
PENCHANT

SHEENA WILDER
THE BRAND VOICE
@PRPrimasInc
"Be Bold & Truthful in Everything you Do and You'll Achieve the Desired Outcome"

DISCOVER THEIR STORIES . #EVOLVINGBEAUTY

Women who courageously surrendered the life they had, to create the life they wanted. Women with unique journeys. They share wisdom, passion & pain points in **THE PLANNER,** Essential Tactics to Being Happy & Successful.
A Self & Brand Mastery Lifestyle Planner.

Independently, each of these women can enterprise and inspire on their own. Collectively they are a tour de force. Women with universal goals, in pursuit to **BEING HAPPY & SUCCESSFUL.**

3.0 THE PERFECT COMBINATION

THE ART OF being happy & successful is a beautiful balancing act that every busy woman strives for. Unfortunately, there just isn't one magic formula. Being happy and successful are evolving pursuits. It requires tuning and fine-tuning, adjustment and re-adjustments, as life evolves.

Being Happy & Successful is a journey, fundamentally rooted in our sense of self and core values. The continual leveling-up to your dreams, wants needs and achievements that create YOUR kind of individual happy. Your kind of indie success.

Success is often associated with making or having a lot of money. The stature and quality of life associated with being rich or wealthy. Let's be honest, who doesn't want to be wealthy and live a life of luxury? Very few do not. If you're convinced that making or having a lot of money is what deems a success. You may be setting yourself up for failure.

Success is not a sprint, it's a marathon. An evolving journey with rich highs and lows presented as lessons for growth. Experiences that build skill sets, networks, businesses, careers, even families.

The Planner was conceived from seeing so many successful people, so unhappy, over the years. People that seemingly have it all financially. All the money success can buy. But they still, aren't happy. In fact, some of the wealthiest people I've ever met were miserable.

Their personal lives were a mess, they were mean and nasty, and their business became "work or worse a managerial game." Those attributes aren't the making of happy people. Successful? Perhaps? Happy? No.

YOUR JOURNEY TO SUCCESS

With different cultural and socio-economic backgrounds. How can the accumulation of wealth and education be the "same "gold standard for everyone? Success is only determined by YOU. Society, family, friends, peers or the illusion of social media do not define success. Today, our culture is inundated with women #BOSSES #BOSS-BABES #BOSS-CHICS, #GIRLBOSSES, etc…Following these trends with the inkling to compete and compare, can become numbing. A business model for failure, disappointment, and unhappiness. The reality is, everyone has their own time and space to achieve and succeed. Success is subjective and personal.

Success is the achievement of something desired, planned or attempted, according to Dictionary.com. This means success is determined and established by YOU. The achievement of YOUR goals define success. The concept of success is simplistic--**you can actually set your definition of success by YOUR own personal goals when you achieve them, you create success.** At least for that milestone…so simple, yet brilliant! That is what success is, a journey, small, consistent milestones of achievement.

DREAM BIG, SHINE BRIGHTLY!

The BIGGER you think, dream and imagine, the more satisfying your achievements will become. It is this stretch of our goals that help support fulfillment.

BEING HAPPY IS A CHOICE

Our culture is somewhat obsessed with the concept of happy. We live in a time where opportunity and choice are greater than it has ever been. As much as I believe we need to be happy, there are points in our life that we must do what we have to do, in order to get to do what we want to do, later. This part of goal setting, is the growth, the pursuit.

Now that you've established that setting extraordinary goals and achieving them are perhaps the most critical component to YOUR personal journey to success, let's explore the other critical component. Happiness.

BEING HAPPY

Happy is an emotional state of pleasure, joy, bliss, enjoyment, delight. Educators and philosophers have debated and sought to define happiness for ages. There is much debate over the definition of happiness, but what philosophers, theologians, and other educators do agree upon, is that just as success is fluid, so is happiness, it is ever evolving, it changes. Continual adjustments and fine-tuning is required.

Women comprise 30% of business owners in the U.S., (The State of Women, 2015) women of color are the fastest growing segment of those entrepreneurs. Building a business requires an enormous investment. Time, passion, money, being away from loved ones. It's is a serious investment. Pursue your dreams with vigor! While investing a large amount of time in being successful, let's make sure we're happy…too.

GETTING STARTED

It is highly recommended that you spend the allotted hour to complete the 4-Step Brand Mastery Worksheet before using THE PLANNER. Identifying your personal core value insertions are critical components to being Happy & Successful!

#BoosttheEvolution.

3.1 THE POWER OF PEN TO PAPER

"Simply writing down your goals in life is the first step toward achieving them,"

Henriette Anne Klauser, Ph.D.
Author of *Write It Down, Make It Happen*

I LOVE TECHNOLOGY. A lot. So much so that I wrote a book about it in 2016. Evolving Beauty®, The Business of Beauty in a New Age. The culture of the digital age is fast. Quick access with rapid-speed two-way engagements full of content to inform, engage and entertain.

Writing pen to paper versus typing slows down the thinking process. It lets you feel each letter, word and the intention of each sentence. Especially useful when setting goals. Writing stimulates a cluster of cells at the base of the brain called the reticular activating system (RAS). According to Innovate Us, a sustainable and practical living service organization, RAS is the place where your thoughts, internal feelings, and the outside influences unite. With this combination, there is no better way to get clear about your goals than the power of pen to paper.

When we write pen to paper versus typing it creates a different relationship between the brain, the written words and the intention of words to goal setting. It is the power of writing, the words of pen to paper that connect to the brain, and their release into the universe that sets vigorous commitment.

Enjoy every day of your year as you set, plan and smash your goals. You deserve it.

3.2 IMPORTANT DATES

JANUARY

National Hot Tea Month
National Mentoring Month

01 - New Year's Day
07 – Zora Neale Hurston's Birthday
11 – National Human Trafficking Awareness Day
14 – National Vision Board Day
16 – Dr. MLK Jr. Day/Civil Rights Day
16 – National Religious Freedom Day
16 – Sugar Awareness Week
26 – National Green Juice Day
28 – Chinese New Year

FEBRUARY

Black History Month

01 – National Freedom Day
02 – Ground Hog Day
04 – Rosa Parks Day
09 – Alice Walker's Birthday
14 - Valentine's Day

MARCH

Women's History Month

01 – Lent Begins
05 – Celebrate Your Name Week
07 – National Be Heard Day
08 – International Women's Day
09 – National Get Over It Day
10 – National Women & Girls HIV/AIDS Awareness Day
12 - Daylight Savings Time Starts
12 – National Plant a Flower Day
16 – National Everything You Do Is Right Day
17 – World Sleep Day
17 – St. Patrick's Day
20 – March Equinox
20 - International Day of Happiness Day 26 – National Cleaning Week
31 – Cesar Chavez Day

APRIL

Women's Health Month

International Balance Month

01 – April Fool's Day
04 – Maya Angelou's Birthday
07 – World Health Day
09 – Palm Sunday
14 – Good Friday
16 - Easter
17 – Take Our Daughters to Work Day 18 – Tax Day
22 – Earth Day
23 – National Take a Chance Day
29 – International Dance Day

IMPORTANT DATES

MAY

Mother's Month

05 – Cinco de Mayo
World Asthma Day – 1st Tuesday
National Anxiety & Depression Awareness Week
National Day of Prayer – 1st Thursday
07 – Teacher Appreciation Week
14 - Mother's Day
25 – National Missing Children's Day
27 – Ramadan Starts
29 – Memorial Day

JUNE

Beauty Music Month

06 – A'Lelia Walker's Birthday
18 – Father's Day
19 – Juneteenth
19 – Emancipation Day
21 – June Solstice

JULY

04 – Independence Day
23 – Parent's Day

AUGUST

06 – Friendship Day
09 – Annie Malone's Birthday
21 – National Aviation Day
26 – Women's Equality Day

SEPTEMBER

04 - Labor Day
11 – Patriot Day
17 – Citizen Day
22 – September Equinox

OCTOBER

02 – Child Health Day
09 – Native America's Day / Indigenous People's Day
16 – Boss's Day
31 - Halloween

NOVEMBER

Beauty Innovation Month

05 – Day Light Savings Ends
07 – Election Day
23 – Thanksgiving Day
24 – American Indian Heritage Day
24 – President's Day
24 – Black Friday

DECEMBER

23 – Madame CJ Walker Birthday
24 – Christmas Eve
25 – Christmas Day
26 – Kwanzaa Starts & Ends – Jan 1
31 – New Year's Eve

POSITIVE PATTERNS

TO PRIORITIZE DAILY

PERSONAL	PROFESSIONAL	PHYSICAL
*Create a daily spiritual practice. Pray/Meditate Daily/Reflection	* Research business: competitors, the industry, new business models, new opportunities.	* Seek & understand the mind, body spirit connection.
*Embrace Change.	* Create win/win business partnerships.	* Exercise
*Prioritize & make time for family, friends.	* Ask for help and support.	* Limit Vices
* Talk about ideas, NOT people.	* Accept the blame for all (company) mistakes.	* Take care of mental health.
* Create a support system	*Learn from others, life learners.	* Maintain a healthy diet: less processed foods, more fruit & vegetables.
* Support family & friends.	* Support other women.	* Get annual exams
* Surround yourself with positive people.	* Share data and information with other women.	* Don't allow three (3)days go by without working out.
* They believe and expect to succeed.	* Work in integrity.	* Make time for mental reflection.
* Ask for help and support.	* Stay in motion – intentional motion. Focused and purposeful aligned with Brand Mastery Priorities (Step 1).	* Have workout partners
* Invest in their future for themselves and their family.	* Take Action- they don't wait for them happen.	* Drink lots of water, limit other drinks, sodas, fruit juices.
* Plan for the future, but don't obsess about it.	* Create a supportive professional network.	
* Are life learners.	* Invest in themselves to learn the skills they need.	
* Maintain a journal.	*Maintain a mentor at all ages.	
* Exude Joy.	* Embrace Change.	
* Schedule time for fun. entertainment, being social.	* Maintain "to do" and "to be" lists.	
* Schedule vacation time.	* Set BIG Goals: daily , monthly , yearly victories - they lead to big successes.	
* Remember the purpose of the journey.	* Set life goals.	
* Accept responsibility for failures.	* Read daily	
* Operate in Integrity.	* Trust intuition	
	* Believe in themselves.	
	* Seek greatness	

Today,_____
(date)

I_____
(name)

am ready to surrender the life I have,

to create the life I want!

I'm prepared to be vulnerable and authentic.

Willing to transform my big dreams into bold goals.

Set for the self-discipline required to create positive life patterns. Patterns

intended for my greatness, to evolve to my level of Happy & Successful!

BRAND & SELF MASTERY WORKSHEETS

THE 3P'S TO BRAND MASTERY

This step is an excerpt from the popular Evolving Beauty® BRAND MASTERY e-worksheet. Goal: Identify authentic core values and align them with your business. When core values of passion, purpose, and profits are aligned, you're on the path to "YOUR" BRAND MASTERY.

Steps 1-4, Recommended Time: 1 Hour

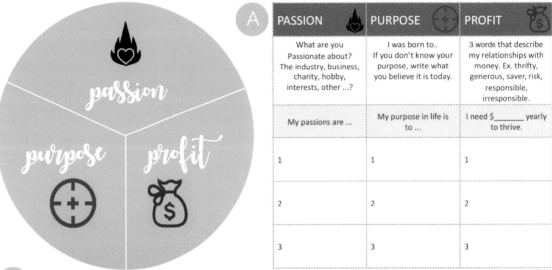

A

PASSION	PURPOSE	PROFIT
What are you Passionate about? The industry, business, charity, hobby, interests, other ...?	I was born to.. If you don't know your purpose, write what you believe it is today.	3 words that describe my relationships with money. Ex. thrifty, generous, saver, risk, responsible, irresponsible.
My passions are ...	My purpose in life is to ...	I need $_____ yearly to thrive.
1	1	1
2	2	2
3	3	3

B

RATE BY IMPORTANCE - 1st, 2nd & 3rd
How will these categories lead your life?

PASSION   PURPOSE   PROFIT

Our original worksheet includes an internal and external SWOT analysis, plus a brand essence and relect and mesaure section. Contact Shine Beauty Culture.com for more info.

C

THE BUSINESS I AM IN IS...

MY POINT OF DIFFERENCE IS...

THE SPECIFIC BUSINESS CATEGORY IS ...

THE 3P'S TO YEARLY GROWTH

STEP 2

This step is to identify where you are, your BIG GOALS--where you want to go with tactics to get there. Goal: Set your personal, professional and physical goals by priorities. How do you want to grow? Be better.

ANNUAL GOAL TIPS

* Set BIG GOALS for each category.

* Streamline to 3 focus areas per category, per year. Small milestones, big goals!

* Set quantitative (#) goals. Example: Work out 3x per week, have lunch with Mom once a month, complete 2 certificate business programs, etc..

* Be creative with growth, create a **BIG** stretch. The larger the goal, the larger the sense of accomplishment and journey to success.

Add category topics that are important to your life.

Complete the Top 3 PHYSICAL GOALS for the year.

WHERE YOU ARE NOW	BIG GOAL	TACTICS TO REACH THE GOAL	FEARS / OBSTACLES
1			
2			
3			

Complete the Top 3 PERSONAL GOALS for the year.

WHERE YOU ARE NOW	BIG GOAL	TACTICS TO REACH THE GOAL	FEARS / OBSTACLES
1			
2			
3			

Complete the Top 3 PROFESSIONAL GOALS for the year.

WHERE YOU ARE NOW	BIG GOAL	TACTICS TO REACH THE GOAL	FEARS / OBSTACLES
1			
2			
3			

ALIGNING BRAND MASTERY PRIORITIES & BUSINESS GOALS

STEP 3

This Step aligns your core values with your business goals to streamline your Brand Mastery priorities.

A

| RATE THE CATEGORIES BY IMPORTANCE IN YOU LIFE. 1 being the most important, then 2 and 3. |
| Rate the categories by how you want these values to lead your life. |

PASSION

PURPOSE

PROFIT

Our original worksheet includes an internal and external SWOT analysis, plus a brand essence and relect & mesasure section. Contact Shine Beauty Culture.com for more info.

B

MY BUSINESS - THE CORE ELEMENTS OF MY BUSINESS ARE...

1

2

3

C

ANSWER THE FOLLOWING QUESTIONS HONESTLY

YES	NO	My business is innovative, forward-thinking, and distinct from most other companies in my category.
YES	NO	My business is completely innovative and new. Something consumers don't know they need..yet. Ex. Apple Watch, iPads, FitBit, airbrush foundation, gel nails, chrome nails, tan lotion, etc..
YES	NO	My business is filling a void that people want.
YES	NO	My business is filling a void that people need.

D

CRITICAL THINKING

___YES - My Brand Mastery priorities (passion, purpose & profit) ARE with my core business goals.
___NO - See note below.

NOTE

If your Brand Mastery priorities (the 3 P's) are NOT aligned with your business goals--continue to assess your "type" of business venture/goal. It does NOT mean you are NOT on your journey or path. It may be a milestone in your evolution. An awaiting change to come. You may perhaps be financially fulfilled, but likely unhappy. A, B, C & D should align.

WRITE YOUR PERSONAL STATEMENT FOR THE YEAR

STEP 4

This Step is to identify where you are now, what your BIG GOALS are and the tactics to get there. How do you want to grow? Be better next year!

PASSION

PURPOSE

PROFIT

A

Spend time developing your personal statement for the year. It should reflect your Brand Mastery Priorities (core values). Refer to Step 3a. Use your priorities to craft your PERSONAL STATEMENT (PS) OF THE YEAR.

1 to 2 sentences, maximum. Examples.

1) This is the year of "me" to handle my life in strength.

2) I have talents the universe needs. I must stretch to discover and monetize them.

3) Only what I need and love.

4) Quality vs. Quantity.

5) Everyday lived like my last to love & share with my tribe.

MY PERSONAL "STATEMENT OF THE YEAR" IS...

B

Use your personal statement to stay focused. Recite daily, it eliminates distractions and reinforces your focus. Write your personal statement at the top of the monthly calendar when you develop your monthly goals.

NOTES

ROCHELLE GRAHAM
THE BEAUTY EMPRESS

"Always be true to yourself. Remember who you are and where you're from."

FOUNDER + CEO

ROCHELLE GRAHAM

Forged into the beauty industry through social media. Known as Vlogger @BlackOnyx77. Today, Black Onyx World, LLC is home to brands created from beauty marketplace misses. Rochelle saw the voids as opportunities, and in only seven short years, Graham has built an empire that will shock, awe and inspire.

My morning routine is...
Meditation/Prayer. I also read something educational or inspirational before I shuffle my little one off to school.

I started my own business because...
I saw that something was missing in this [beauty] industry, so I decided I wanted to fill the void.

Early on what were your hardest business challenges?
I overcame it by...
The hardest challenges were finances, having enough manpower and time. I overcame finances by getting a second job to fund our business.

We overcame manpower by hiring friends and family because they allowed us to pay them with products. We overcame time by sacrificing extracurricular activities to focus on my business.

I love the beauty industry because...
The beauty industry is always evolving and changing. You can make an impact on someone's life beyond the surface-self-esteem, self-worth and self-confidence.

How has the Digital Age changed your business?
The Digital Age has changed my business in many positive ways. Without YouTube, I wouldn't be able to share my journey or my products. The low side is that social media can perpetuate negative information, business or personal.

I AM
CREATIVE
DETERMINED
+ FABULOUS

THE BEAUTY EMPRESS

"Work Hard for Everything, Expect Nothing."

BLACK ONYX WORLD, LLC
is the home of

- **Alikay Naturals** - A luxury natural and organic hair, skin, bath and body line,

- **Be Fabulous Salon**-Southwest Florida's premiere natural salon and spa,

- **BlackOnyx77** - A Fashion, Beauty and Lifestyle Vlog.

- **Mogul University** – Everything Business School Didn't Teach You.

© EvolvingBeauty.Info

Rochelle is a native of Montego Bay, Jamaica. She has a Business Marketing degree from the University of South Florida. She and her family reside in Ft. Meyers, Florida. For more information go to AlikayNaturals.com, @AlikayNaturals, @BlackOnyx77.

EVOLVING BEAUTY

THE PLANNER
ESSENTIAL TACTICS TO BEING
happy
& SUCCESSFUL

MONTH:

MY PERSONAL STATEMENT FOR THE YEAR

What you are seeking is seeking you. –Rumi

SUNDAY	MONDAY	TUESDAY	WEDNESDAY	THURSDAY	FRIDAY	SATURDAY

Visualize the completion of your Personal, Professional and Physical goals.
*Your monthly goals should align with your **Brand Mastery Priorities** from Step 1.*

My Personal Intention is…
1
2
3

My Professional Intention is…
1
2
3

My Physical Intention is…
1
2
3

GRATITUDES/NOTES

DATE:

THIS WEEK'S GOAL

EVOLVING
BEAUTY

THE PLANNER
ESSENTIAL TACTICS TO BEING
happy
&
SUCCESSFUL

THIS WEEK'S PRIORITIES	MONDAY	TUESDAY	WEDNESDAY
	TODAY'S GOAL	TODAY'S GOAL	TODAY'S GOAL
	PRIORITIES	PRIORITIES	PRIORITIES
	1	1	1
	2	2	2
	3	3	3
	4am	4am	4am
	5am	5am	5am
	6am	6am	6am
	7am	7am	7am
	8am	8am	8am
	9am	9am	9am
	10am	10am	10am
	11am	11am	11am
	12am	12am	12am
	1pm	1pm	1pm
	2pm	2pm	2pm
	3pm	3pm	3pm
	4pm	4pm	4pm
	5pm	5pm	5pm
	6pm	6pm	6pm
	7pm	7pm	7pm
	9pm	9pm	9pm
	10pm	10pm	10pm

ERRANDS

POSITIVE PATTERNS

	S	M	T	W	T	F	S
PHYSICAL							
PERSONAL							
PROFESSIONAL							

THE PLANNER

ESSENTIAL TACTICS TO BEING

happy

&
SUCCESSFUL

THURSDAY		FRIDAY		SATURDAY		SUNDAY	
TODAY'S GOAL		TODAY'S GOAL		TODAY'S GOAL		TODAY'S GOAL	
PRIORITIES		PRIORITIES		PRIORITIES		PRIORITIES	
1		1		1		1	
2		2		2		2	
3		3		3		3	
4am		4am		4am		4am	
5am		5am		5am		5am	
6am		6am		6am		6am	
7am		7am		7am		7am	
8am		8am		8am		8am	
9am		9am		9am		9am	
10am		10am		10am		10am	
11am		11am		11am		11am	
12am		12am		12am		12am	
1pm		1pm		1pm		1pm	
2pm		2pm		2pm		2pm	
3pm		3pm		3pm		3pm	
4pm		4pm		4pm		4pm	
5pm		5pm		5pm		5pm	
6pm		6pm		6pm		6pm	
7pm		7pm		7pm		7pm	
9pm		9pm		9pm		9pm	
10pm		10pm		10pm		10pm	

DISTRACTIONS THIS WEEK	BIG IDEAS THIS WEEK

DATE:

THIS WEEK'S GOAL

EVOLVING BEAUTY

THE PLANNER
ESSENTIAL TACTICS TO BEING
happy
& SUCCESSFUL

THIS WEEK'S PRIORITIES	MONDAY	TUESDAY	WEDNESDAY
	TODAY'S GOAL	TODAY'S GOAL	TODAY'S GOAL
	PRIORITIES	PRIORITIES	PRIORITIES
	1	1	1
	2	2	2
	3	3	3
	4am	4am	4am
	5am	5am	5am
	6am	6am	6am
	7am	7am	7am
	8am	8am	8am
	9am	9am	9am
	10am	10am	10am
	11am	11am	11am
	12am	12am	12am
	1pm	1pm	1pm
	2pm	2pm	2pm
	3pm	3pm	3pm
	4pm	4pm	4pm
	5pm	5pm	5pm
	6pm	6pm	6pm
	7pm	7pm	7pm
	9pm	9pm	9pm
	10pm	10pm	10pm

ERRANDS

POSITIVE PATTERNS

	S	M	T	W	T	F	S
PHYSICAL							
PERSONAL							
PROFESSIONAL							

THE PLANNER

ESSENTIAL TACTICS TO BEING

happy

& SUCCESSFUL

THURSDAY		FRIDAY		SATURDAY		SUNDAY	
TODAY'S GOAL		TODAY'S GOAL		TODAY'S GOAL		TODAY'S GOAL	
PRIORITIES		PRIORITIES		PRIORITIES		PRIORITIES	
1		1		1		1	
2		2		2		2	
3		3		3		3	
4am		4am		4am		4am	
5am		5am		5am		5am	
6am		6am		6am		6am	
7am		7am		7am		7am	
8am		8am		8am		8am	
9am		9am		9am		9am	
10am		10am		10am		10am	
11am		11am		11am		11am	
12am		12am		12am		12am	
1pm		1pm		1pm		1pm	
2pm		2pm		2pm		2pm	
3pm		3pm		3pm		3pm	
4pm		4pm		4pm		4pm	
5pm		5pm		5pm		5pm	
6pm		6pm		6pm		6pm	
7pm		7pm		7pm		7pm	
9pm		9pm		9pm		9pm	
10pm		10pm		10pm		10pm	

DISTRACTIONS THIS WEEK	BIG IDEAS THIS WEEK

DATE:

THIS WEEK'S GOAL

THIS WEEK'S PRIORITIES	MONDAY	TUESDAY	WEDNESDAY
	TODAY'S GOAL	TODAY'S GOAL	TODAY'S GOAL
	PRIORITIES	PRIORITIES	PRIORITIES
	1	1	1
	2	2	2
	3	3	3
	4am	4am	4am
	5am	5am	5am
	6am	6am	6am
	7am	7am	7am
	8am	8am	8am
	9am	9am	9am
	10am	10am	10am
	11am	11am	11am
	12am	12am	12am
	1pm	1pm	1pm
	2pm	2pm	2pm
	3pm	3pm	3pm
	4pm	4pm	4pm
	5pm	5pm	5pm
	6pm	6pm	6pm
	7pm	7pm	7pm
	9pm	9pm	9pm
	10pm	10pm	10pm

ERRANDS

POSITIVE PATTERNS	S	M	T	W	T	F	S
PHYSICAL							
PERSONAL							
PROFESSIONAL							

THE PLANNER

ESSENTIAL TACTICS TO BEING

happy
& SUCCESSFUL

THURSDAY		FRIDAY		SATURDAY		SUNDAY	
TODAY'S GOAL		TODAY'S GOAL		TODAY'S GOAL		TODAY'S GOAL	
PRIORITIES		PRIORITIES		PRIORITIES		PRIORITIES	
1		1		1		1	
2		2		2		2	
3		3		3		3	
4am		4am		4am		4am	
5am		5am		5am		5am	
6am		6am		6am		6am	
7am		7am		7am		7am	
8am		8am		8am		8am	
9am		9am		9am		9am	
10am		10am		10am		10am	
11am		11am		11am		11am	
12am		12am		12am		12am	
1pm		1pm		1pm		1pm	
2pm		2pm		2pm		2pm	
3pm		3pm		3pm		3pm	
4pm		4pm		4pm		4pm	
5pm		5pm		5pm		5pm	
6pm		6pm		6pm		6pm	
7pm		7pm		7pm		7pm	
9pm		9pm		9pm		9pm	
10pm		10pm		10pm		10pm	

DISTRACTIONS THIS WEEK	BIG IDEAS THIS WEEK

DATE:

THIS WEEK'S GOAL

THIS WEEK'S PRIORITIES	MONDAY	TUESDAY	WEDNESDAY
	TODAY'S GOAL	TODAY'S GOAL	TODAY'S GOAL

	PRIORITIES	PRIORITIES	PRIORITIES
	1	1	1
	2	2	2
	3	3	3
	4am	4am	4am
	5am	5am	5am
	6am	6am	6am
	7am	7am	7am
	8am	8am	8am
	9am	9am	9am
	10am	10am	10am
	11am	11am	11am
	12am	12am	12am
	1pm	1pm	1pm
	2pm	2pm	2pm
	3pm	3pm	3pm
	4pm	4pm	4pm
	5pm	5pm	5pm
	6pm	6pm	6pm
	7pm	7pm	7pm
	9pm	9pm	9pm
	10pm	10pm	10pm

ERRANDS

POSITIVE PATTERNS

	S	M	T	W	T	F	S
PHYSICAL							
PERSONAL							
PROFESSIONAL							

THE PLANNER

ESSENTIAL TACTICS TO BEING

happy
& SUCCESSFUL

THURSDAY		FRIDAY		SATURDAY		SUNDAY	
TODAY'S GOAL		TODAY'S GOAL		TODAY'S GOAL		TODAY'S GOAL	
PRIORITIES		PRIORITIES		PRIORITIES		PRIORITIES	
1		1		1		1	
2		2		2		2	
3		3		3		3	
4am		4am		4am		4am	
5am		5am		5am		5am	
6am		6am		6am		6am	
7am		7am		7am		7am	
8am		8am		8am		8am	
9am		9am		9am		9am	
10am		10am		10am		10am	
11am		11am		11am		11am	
12am		12am		12am		12am	
1pm		1pm		1pm		1pm	
2pm		2pm		2pm		2pm	
3pm		3pm		3pm		3pm	
4pm		4pm		4pm		4pm	
5pm		5pm		5pm		5pm	
6pm		6pm		6pm		6pm	
7pm		7pm		7pm		7pm	
9pm		9pm		9pm		9pm	
10pm		10pm		10pm		10pm	

DISTRACTIONS THIS WEEK	BIG IDEAS THIS WEEK

DATE:

THIS WEEK'S GOAL

EVOLVING
BEAUTY

THE PLANNER
ESSENTIAL TACTICS TO BEING

happy
&
SUCCESSFUL

THIS WEEK'S PRIORITIES	MONDAY	TUESDAY	WEDNESDAY
	TODAY'S GOAL	TODAY'S GOAL	TODAY'S GOAL
	PRIORITIES	PRIORITIES	PRIORITIES
	1	1	1
	2	2	2
	3	3	3
	4am	4am	4am
	5am	5am	5am
	6am	6am	6am
	7am	7am	7am
	8am	8am	8am
	9am	9am	9am
	10am	10am	10am
	11am	11am	11am
	12am	12am	12am
	1pm	1pm	1pm
	2pm	2pm	2pm
	3pm	3pm	3pm
	4pm	4pm	4pm
	5pm	5pm	5pm
	6pm	6pm	6pm
	7pm	7pm	7pm
	9pm	9pm	9pm
	10pm	10pm	10pm

ERRANDS

POSITIVE PATTERNS

	S	M	T	W	T	F	S
PHYSICAL							
PERSONAL							
PROFESSIONAL							

THE PLANNER
ESSENTIAL TACTICS TO BEING
happy
& SUCCESSFUL

THURSDAY		FRIDAY		SATURDAY		SUNDAY	
TODAY'S GOAL		TODAY'S GOAL		TODAY'S GOAL		TODAY'S GOAL	
PRIORITIES		PRIORITIES		PRIORITIES		PRIORITIES	
1		1		1		1	
2		2		2		2	
3		3		3		3	
4am		4am		4am		4am	
5am		5am		5am		5am	
6am		6am		6am		6am	
7am		7am		7am		7am	
8am		8am		8am		8am	
9am		9am		9am		9am	
10am		10am		10am		10am	
11am		11am		11am		11am	
12am		12am		12am		12am	
1pm		1pm		1pm		1pm	
2pm		2pm		2pm		2pm	
3pm		3pm		3pm		3pm	
4pm		4pm		4pm		4pm	
5pm		5pm		5pm		5pm	
6pm		6pm		6pm		6pm	
7pm		7pm		7pm		7pm	
9pm		9pm		9pm		9pm	
10pm		10pm		10pm		10pm	

DISTRACTIONS THIS WEEK	BIG IDEAS THIS WEEK

MONTHLY REFLECTION

Visualize, in gratitude, Achieving Your Goals
*Use the senses to see, hear, smell,
and touch the experience of what your success will look and feel like.*

	MONTHLY GOAL		ACHIEVEMENT
1			
2			
3			

	PERSONAL	TIME SPENT	TACTICS FOR IMPROVEMENT
1			
2			
3			
	PROFESSIONAL		
1			
2			
3			
	PHYSICAL		
1			
2			
3			

1. WHAT DID I LEARN THIS MONTH?
1.
2.
3.
4.
5.

2. DISTRACTIONS AVOID / FEARS TO FORGE THROUGH
1.
2.
3.
4.
5.

3. PEOPLE I LEARNED FROM OR INSPIRED ME?
1.
2.
3.
4.
5.

4. MISSED OPPORTUNITIES THIS MONTH?
1.
2.
3.
4.
5.

5. WHAT ACTIONS CAN I CORRECT FOR NEXT MONTH?
1.
2.
3.
4.
5.

HOW DID I SPENT MY TIME THIS MONTH?
** KEEP BRAND MASTERY PRIORITIES &
PERSONAL STATEMENT TOP OF MIND.*
WHAT YOU SAY AND DO SHOULD ALIGN.

PERSONAL
___% Time

PROFESSIONAL
___% Time

PHYSICAL
___% Time

32

NOTES

TANESHA BARNES
BEAUTY'S FREEDOM FIGHTER

"When you see the beauty in yourself, you walk the earth differently."

FOUNDER

LICENSED ESTHETICIAN + CEO

T. Barnes

A LIFESTYLE OF BEAUTY

TANESHA BARNES

Is on a mission to connect, protect, and beautify women of color from the inside out. She is committed to creating economic, intellectual and spiritual bridges for women from the African Diaspora. Unapologetic about her beliefs. Unbothered by the notion of financial compromise from those opposing her stance. She leverages her passion--her exquisitely made, natural-based products as a bridge to her purpose. TaNesha is BEAUTY'S FREEDOM FIGHTER. Trust, the beauty industry and women of the world will thank T. Barnes. Ase`.

My business is distinct because...
T. Barnes Beauty is distinct because my product portfolio has a vegan foundation, I'm also a Licensed Esthetician. All ingredients are organic or mineral-based. Everything that I do is rooted beyond beauty. The products I create have [intentional] healing in the ingredients.

My morning routine is... Up at 5 am, I work best from 5–7:30 am before taking my kid to school.

My personal mantra is... I live by a code of standards, a certain set of politics that guide my life. I don't sway from them. I'm not trending; My life is not governed by popularity or money. Keeping true to who I am is what people buy into from me. And the goodness of T.Barnes Beauty products. My products are really, really good.

I would tell my younger self about being an entrepreneur... Bring your "A" Game and discipline yourself. When I was younger, I was really good at entrepreneurship, but didn't take it seriously. The discipline required has to be developed earlier, than later.

I want my legacy to be... I hope when people look at my legacy they see me as a freedom fighter, to feed us...To help [return] us (people of color) back to ourselves.

I believe in the future the beauty industry will include... I would like the beauty industry to be healthier [in their messaging]. To use a [marketing] model that builds up to sell, versus highlighting what women lack. A "Be Beautiful" type of stance, that won't cause cancer or lower a woman's self-esteem. I want black women to continue to set the trends in the industry, to support our $10 Million plus, annual spend.

I AM
FOCUSED
A WARRIOR
+ LOVER OF HUMANITY

"I'm willing to partner long-term with people that may not have the best service. But, have the highest integrity. I trust we can get better together."

Organic Skincare, Bath and Body products. Vegan Cosmetics, Apparel & Retreats.
A LIFESTYLE OF BEAUTY

TaNesha is a native of Austin, TX. She holds a B.A. degree in Sociology (NYU), a B.A. in Social Justice (Marlboro College Vermont), a M.A. in History (Western CT State) and a Licensed Esthetician. She currently lives between Connecticut and Anguilla,, where she has two stores. T. Barnes is manufactured in Africa. For more information go to TBarnesBeauty.com | @TBarnesBeauty.

© EvolvingBeauty.Info

MONTH:

MY PERSONAL STATEMENT FOR THE YEAR

"Every great dream begins with a dreamer." Harriett Tubman

SUNDAY	MONDAY	TUESDAY	WEDNESDAY	THURSDAY	FRIDAY	SATURDAY

GRATITUDES/NOTES

Visualize the completion of your Personal, Professional and Physical goals.
*Your monthly goals should align with your **Brand Mastery Priorities** from Step 1.*

My Personal Intention is...
1
2
3

My Professional Intention is...
1
2
3

My Physical Intention is...
1
2
3

DATE:

THIS WEEK'S GOAL

EVOLVING BEAUTY

THE PLANNER
ESSENTIAL TACTICS TO BEING
happy
& SUCCESSFUL

THIS WEEK'S PRIORITIES	MONDAY		TUESDAY		WEDNESDAY	
	TODAY'S GOAL		TODAY'S GOAL		TODAY'S GOAL	
	PRIORITIES		PRIORITIES		PRIORITIES	
	1		1		1	
	2		2		2	
	3		3		3	
	4am		4am		4am	
	5am		5am		5am	
	6am		6am		6am	
	7am		7am		7am	
	8am		8am		8am	
	9am		9am		9am	
	10am		10am		10am	
	11am		11am		11am	
	12am		12am		12am	
	1pm		1pm		1pm	
	2pm		2pm		2pm	
	3pm		3pm		3pm	
	4pm		4pm		4pm	
	5pm		5pm		5pm	
	6pm		6pm		6pm	
	7pm		7pm		7pm	
	9pm		9pm		9pm	
	10pm		10pm		10pm	

ERRANDS

POSITIVE PATTERNS

	S	M	T	W	T	F	S
PHYSICAL							
PERSONAL							
PROFESSIONAL							

THURSDAY		FRIDAY		SATURDAY		SUNDAY	
TODAY'S GOAL		TODAY'S GOAL		TODAY'S GOAL		TODAY'S GOAL	
PRIORITIES		PRIORITIES		PRIORITIES		PRIORITIES	
1		1		1		1	
2		2		2		2	
3		3		3		3	
4am		4am		4am		4am	
5am		5am		5am		5am	
6am		6am		6am		6am	
7am		7am		7am		7am	
8am		8am		8am		8am	
9am		9am		9am		9am	
10am		10am		10am		10am	
11am		11am		11am		11am	
12am		12am		12am		12am	
1pm		1pm		1pm		1pm	
2pm		2pm		2pm		2pm	
3pm		3pm		3pm		3pm	
4pm		4pm		4pm		4pm	
5pm		5pm		5pm		5pm	
6pm		6pm		6pm		6pm	
7pm		7pm		7pm		7pm	
9pm		9pm		9pm		9pm	
10pm		10pm		10pm		10pm	

DISTRACTIONS THIS WEEK	BIG IDEAS THIS WEEK

DATE:

THIS WEEK'S GOAL

THE PLANNER
ESSENTIAL TACTICS TO BEING
happy
&
SUCCESSFUL

THIS WEEK'S PRIORITIES	MONDAY	TUESDAY	WEDNESDAY
	TODAY'S GOAL	TODAY'S GOAL	TODAY'S GOAL
	PRIORITIES	PRIORITIES	PRIORITIES
	1	1	1
	2	2	2
	3	3	3
	4am	4am	4am
	5am	5am	5am
	6am	6am	6am
	7am	7am	7am
	8am	8am	8am
	9am	9am	9am
	10am	10am	10am
	11am	11am	11am
	12am	12am	12am
	1pm	1pm	1pm
	2pm	2pm	2pm
	3pm	3pm	3pm
	4pm	4pm	4pm
	5pm	5pm	5pm
	6pm	6pm	6pm
	7pm	7pm	7pm
	9pm	9pm	9pm
	10pm	10pm	10pm

ERRANDS

POSITIVE PATTERNS	S	M	T	W	T	F	S
PHYSICAL							
PERSONAL							
PROFESSIONAL							

40

THE PLANNER

ESSENTIAL TACTICS TO BEING

happy
& SUCCESSFUL

THURSDAY		FRIDAY		SATURDAY		SUNDAY	
TODAY'S GOAL		TODAY'S GOAL		TODAY'S GOAL		TODAY'S GOAL	
PRIORITIES		PRIORITIES		PRIORITIES		PRIORITIES	
1		1		1		1	
2		2		2		2	
3		3		3		3	
4am		4am		4am		4am	
5am		5am		5am		5am	
6am		6am		6am		6am	
7am		7am		7am		7am	
8am		8am		8am		8am	
9am		9am		9am		9am	
10am		10am		10am		10am	
11am		11am		11am		11am	
12am		12am		12am		12am	
1pm		1pm		1pm		1pm	
2pm		2pm		2pm		2pm	
3pm		3pm		3pm		3pm	
4pm		4pm		4pm		4pm	
5pm		5pm		5pm		5pm	
6pm		6pm		6pm		6pm	
7pm		7pm		7pm		7pm	
9pm		9pm		9pm		9pm	
10pm		10pm		10pm		10pm	

DISTRACTIONS THIS WEEK	BIG IDEAS THIS WEEK

DATE:

EVOLVING
BEAUTY

THE PLANNER
ESSENTIAL TACTICS TO BEING
happy
&
SUCCESSFUL

THIS WEEK'S PRIORITIES	MONDAY	TUESDAY	WEDNESDAY
	TODAY'S GOAL	TODAY'S GOAL	TODAY'S GOAL
	PRIORITIES	PRIORITIES	PRIORITIES
	1	1	1
	2	2	2
	3	3	3
	4am	4am	4am
	5am	5am	5am
	6am	6am	6am
	7am	7am	7am
	8am	8am	8am
	9am	9am	9am
	10am	10am	10am
	11am	11am	11am
	12am	12am	12am
	1pm	1pm	1pm
	2pm	2pm	2pm
	3pm	3pm	3pm
	4pm	4pm	4pm
	5pm	5pm	5pm
	6pm	6pm	6pm
	7pm	7pm	7pm
	9pm	9pm	9pm
	10pm	10pm	10pm

ERRANDS	POSITIVE PATTERNS						
		S	M	T	W	T	F	S
	PHYSICAL							
	PERSONAL							
	PROFESSIONAL							

THE PLANNER
ESSENTIAL TACTICS TO BEING
happy
& SUCCESSFUL

THURSDAY		FRIDAY		SATURDAY		SUNDAY	
TODAY'S GOAL		TODAY'S GOAL		TODAY'S GOAL		TODAY'S GOAL	
PRIORITIES		PRIORITIES		PRIORITIES		PRIORITIES	
1		1		1		1	
2		2		2		2	
3		3		3		3	
4am		4am		4am		4am	
5am		5am		5am		5am	
6am		6am		6am		6am	
7am		7am		7am		7am	
8am		8am		8am		8am	
9am		9am		9am		9am	
10am		10am		10am		10am	
11am		11am		11am		11am	
12am		12am		12am		12am	
1pm		1pm		1pm		1pm	
2pm		2pm		2pm		2pm	
3pm		3pm		3pm		3pm	
4pm		4pm		4pm		4pm	
5pm		5pm		5pm		5pm	
6pm		6pm		6pm		6pm	
7pm		7pm		7pm		7pm	
9pm		9pm		9pm		9pm	
10pm		10pm		10pm		10pm	

DISTRACTIONS THIS WEEK	BIG IDEAS THIS WEEK

DATE:

THIS WEEK'S GOAL

EVOLVING BEAUTY

THE PLANNER
ESSENTIAL TACTICS TO BEING
happy
& SUCCESSFUL

THIS WEEK'S PRIORITIES	MONDAY	TUESDAY	WEDNESDAY
	TODAY'S GOAL	TODAY'S GOAL	TODAY'S GOAL

	PRIORITIES	PRIORITIES	PRIORITIES
	1	1	1
	2	2	2
	3	3	3
	4am	4am	4am
	5am	5am	5am
	6am	6am	6am
	7am	7am	7am
	8am	8am	8am
	9am	9am	9am
	10am	10am	10am
	11am	11am	11am
	12am	12am	12am
	1pm	1pm	1pm
	2pm	2pm	2pm
	3pm	3pm	3pm
	4pm	4pm	4pm
	5pm	5pm	5pm
	6pm	6pm	6pm
	7pm	7pm	7pm
	9pm	9pm	9pm
	10pm	10pm	10pm

ERRANDS

POSITIVE PATTERNS

	S	M	T	W	T	F	S
PHYSICAL							
PERSONAL							
PROFESSIONAL							

THE PLANNER
ESSENTIAL TACTICS TO BEING
happy
& SUCCESSFUL

THURSDAY		FRIDAY		SATURDAY		SUNDAY	
TODAY'S GOAL		TODAY'S GOAL		TODAY'S GOAL		TODAY'S GOAL	
PRIORITIES		PRIORITIES		PRIORITIES		PRIORITIES	
1		1		1		1	
2		2		2		2	
3		3		3		3	
4am		4am		4am		4am	
5am		5am		5am		5am	
6am		6am		6am		6am	
7am		7am		7am		7am	
8am		8am		8am		8am	
9am		9am		9am		9am	
10am		10am		10am		10am	
11am		11am		11am		11am	
12am		12am		12am		12am	
1pm		1pm		1pm		1pm	
2pm		2pm		2pm		2pm	
3pm		3pm		3pm		3pm	
4pm		4pm		4pm		4pm	
5pm		5pm		5pm		5pm	
6pm		6pm		6pm		6pm	
7pm		7pm		7pm		7pm	
9pm		9pm		9pm		9pm	
10pm		10pm		10pm		10pm	

DISTRACTIONS THIS WEEK	BIG IDEAS THIS WEEK

DATE:

THIS WEEK'S PRIORITIES	MONDAY	TUESDAY	WEDNESDAY
	TODAY'S GOAL	TODAY'S GOAL	TODAY'S GOAL
	PRIORITIES	PRIORITIES	PRIORITIES
	1	1	1
	2	2	2
	3	3	3
	4am	4am	4am
	5am	5am	5am
	6am	6am	6am
	7am	7am	7am
	8am	8am	8am
	9am	9am	9am
	10am	10am	10am
	11am	11am	11am
	12am	12am	12am
	1pm	1pm	1pm
	2pm	2pm	2pm
	3pm	3pm	3pm
	4pm	4pm	4pm
	5pm	5pm	5pm
	6pm	6pm	6pm
	7pm	7pm	7pm
	9pm	9pm	9pm
	10pm	10pm	10pm

ERRANDS

POSITIVE PATTERNS

	S	M	T	W	T	F	S
PHYSICAL							
PERSONAL							
PROFESSIONAL							

46

THE PLANNER
ESSENTIAL TACTICS TO BEING
happy
& SUCCESSFUL

THURSDAY		FRIDAY		SATURDAY		SUNDAY	
TODAY'S GOAL		TODAY'S GOAL		TODAY'S GOAL		TODAY'S GOAL	
PRIORITIES		PRIORITIES		PRIORITIES		PRIORITIES	
1		1		1		1	
2		2		2		2	
3		3		3		3	
4am		4am		4am		4am	
5am		5am		5am		5am	
6am		6am		6am		6am	
7am		7am		7am		7am	
8am		8am		8am		8am	
9am		9am		9am		9am	
10am		10am		10am		10am	
11am		11am		11am		11am	
12am		12am		12am		12am	
1pm		1pm		1pm		1pm	
2pm		2pm		2pm		2pm	
3pm		3pm		3pm		3pm	
4pm		4pm		4pm		4pm	
5pm		5pm		5pm		5pm	
6pm		6pm		6pm		6pm	
7pm		7pm		7pm		7pm	
9pm		9pm		9pm		9pm	
10pm		10pm		10pm		10pm	

DISTRACTIONS THIS WEEK	BIG IDEAS THIS WEEK

MONTHLY REFLECTION

Visualize, in gratitude, Achieving Your Goals
*Use the senses to see, hear, smell,
and touch the experience of what your success will look and feel like.*

	MONTHLY GOAL	ACHIEVEMENT
1		
2		
3		

	PERSONAL	TIME SPENT	TACTICS FOR IMPROVEMENT
1			
2			
3			
	PROFESSIONAL		
1			
2			
3			
	PHYSICAL		
1			
2			
3			

1. WHAT DID I LEARN THIS MONTH?
1.
2.
3.
4.
5.

2. DISTRACTIONS AVOID / FEARS TO FORGE THROUGH
1.
2.
3.
4.
5.

3. PEOPLE I LEARNED FROM OR INSPIRED ME?
1.
2.
3.
4.
5.

4. MISSED OPPORTUNITIES THIS MONTH?
1.
2.
3.
4.
5.

5. WHAT ACTIONS CAN I CORRECT FOR NEXT MONTH?
1.
2.
3.
4.
5.

HOW DID I SPENT MY TIME THIS MONTH?
* KEEP BRAND MASTERY PRIORITIES &
PERSONAL STATEMENT TOP OF MIND.
WHAT YOU SAY AND DO SHOULD ALIGN.

PERSONAL
___% Time

PROFESSIONAL
___% Time

PHYSICAL
___% Time

NOTES

NOTES

TIFFINI GATLIN
AN EVOLVING INNOVATOR

"*Mistakes and Failures are Preparation for Greater Opportunities.*"

FOUNDER & CEO

LATCHED:HOOKED
everything you need to take your style to the next level

TIFFINI GATLIN

An **EVOLVING INNOVATOR**. She started her first business, braiding hair in her Mom's basement, at 16 years old. An incessant beauty innovator, wife and Mom of four. Check out her latest enterprise on LatchedandHooked.com.

"Don't Stagnate, Innovate. Seek New Ways to Do Business."

LATCHED:HOOKED

My business is distinct because...
I'm 100% woman owned and operated. A black woman designing my own synthetic hair extensions.

On work/life balance... I don't balance, I prioritize.

I love the beauty industry because...
It gives me a direct impact on how a woman feels. If a woman feels and looks her best—she will conquer the world!

My personal mantra...
Honest and poor is better than rich and dishonest. I love a healthy conscious.

I want my legacy to be... I want my legacy to be that I changed the stigma that hair extensions have within the African American Community. I also want to be the first black woman to crack the code on manufacturing hair and bringing it to the United States.

I believe in the future the beauty industry will include.... Beauty retailers emulating grocery stores, with aisles of ingredients available to consumers to create personalized formulas, individual to their needs.

A lifestyle beauty brand that helps women of color achieve flawless hairstyles for up to eight (8) weeks, with the help of our chemical free, textured, synthetic hair extensions.

I AM
A VISIONARY.
**RESILIENT
+DEDICATED**

Tiffini is a native of Baltimore, MD. She holds a B.A. in Public Relations from Clark Atlanta University in Atlanta, Ga.; where she lives with her family. For more information go to LatchedandHooked.com @LatchednHooked.com

MONTH:

MY PERSONAL STATEMENT FOR THE YEAR

"Don't sit down and wait for opportunities to come, get up and make them." - Madame CJ Walker

SUNDAY	MONDAY	TUESDAY	WEDNESDAY	THURSDAY	FRIDAY	SATURDAY

Visualize the completion of your Personal, Professional and Physical goals.
*Your monthly goals should align with your **Brand Mastery Priorities** from Step 1.*

My Personal Intention is...

1

2

3

My Professional Intention is...

1

2

3

My Physical Intention is...

1

2

3

GRATITUDES/NOTES

DATE:

THIS WEEK'S GOAL

THIS WEEK'S PRIORITIES	MONDAY	TUESDAY	WEDNESDAY
	TODAY'S GOAL	TODAY'S GOAL	TODAY'S GOAL
	PRIORITIES	PRIORITIES	PRIORITIES
	1	1	1
	2	2	2
	3	3	3
	4am	4am	4am
	5am	5am	5am
	6am	6am	6am
	7am	7am	7am
	8am	8am	8am
	9am	9am	9am
	10am	10am	10am
	11am	11am	11am
	12am	12am	12am
	1pm	1pm	1pm
	2pm	2pm	2pm
	3pm	3pm	3pm
	4pm	4pm	4pm
	5pm	5pm	5pm
	6pm	6pm	6pm
	7pm	7pm	7pm
	9pm	9pm	9pm
	10pm	10pm	10pm

ERRANDS

POSITIVE PATTERNS

	S	M	T	W	T	F	S
PHYSICAL							
PERSONAL							
PROFESSIONAL							

THE PLANNER

ESSENTIAL TACTICS TO BEING

happy
& SUCCESSFUL

THURSDAY		FRIDAY		SATURDAY		SUNDAY	
TODAY'S GOAL		TODAY'S GOAL		TODAY'S GOAL		TODAY'S GOAL	
PRIORITIES		PRIORITIES		PRIORITIES		PRIORITIES	
1		1		1		1	
2		2		2		2	
3		3		3		3	
4am		4am		4am		4am	
5am		5am		5am		5am	
6am		6am		6am		6am	
7am		7am		7am		7am	
8am		8am		8am		8am	
9am		9am		9am		9am	
10am		10am		10am		10am	
11am		11am		11am		11am	
12am		12am		12am		12am	
1pm		1pm		1pm		1pm	
2pm		2pm		2pm		2pm	
3pm		3pm		3pm		3pm	
4pm		4pm		4pm		4pm	
5pm		5pm		5pm		5pm	
6pm		6pm		6pm		6pm	
7pm		7pm		7pm		7pm	
9pm		9pm		9pm		9pm	
10pm		10pm		10pm		10pm	

DISTRACTIONS THIS WEEK	BIG IDEAS THIS WEEK

DATE:

THIS WEEK'S GOAL

THIS WEEK'S PRIORITIES

MONDAY	TUESDAY	WEDNESDAY
TODAY'S GOAL	TODAY'S GOAL	TODAY'S GOAL

PRIORITIES		PRIORITIES		PRIORITIES	
1		1		1	
2		2		2	
3		3		3	
4am		4am		4am	
5am		5am		5am	
6am		6am		6am	
7am		7am		7am	
8am		8am		8am	
9am		9am		9am	
10am		10am		10am	
11am		11am		11am	
12am		12am		12am	
1pm		1pm		1pm	
2pm		2pm		2pm	
3pm		3pm		3pm	
4pm		4pm		4pm	
5pm		5pm		5pm	
6pm		6pm		6pm	
7pm		7pm		7pm	
9pm		9pm		9pm	
10pm		10pm		10pm	

ERRANDS

POSITIVE PATTERNS							
	S	M	T	W	T	F	S
PHYSICAL							
PERSONAL							
PROFESSIONAL							

THURSDAY		FRIDAY		SATURDAY		SUNDAY	
TODAY'S GOAL		TODAY'S GOAL		TODAY'S GOAL		TODAY'S GOAL	
PRIORITIES		PRIORITIES		PRIORITIES		PRIORITIES	
1		1		1		1	
2		2		2		2	
3		3		3		3	
4am		4am		4am		4am	
5am		5am		5am		5am	
6am		6am		6am		6am	
7am		7am		7am		7am	
8am		8am		8am		8am	
9am		9am		9am		9am	
10am		10am		10am		10am	
11am		11am		11am		11am	
12am		12am		12am		12am	
1pm		1pm		1pm		1pm	
2pm		2pm		2pm		2pm	
3pm		3pm		3pm		3pm	
4pm		4pm		4pm		4pm	
5pm		5pm		5pm		5pm	
6pm		6pm		6pm		6pm	
7pm		7pm		7pm		7pm	
9pm		9pm		9pm		9pm	
10pm		10pm		10pm		10pm	

DISTRACTIONS THIS WEEK	BIG IDEAS THIS WEEK

DATE:

THIS WEEK'S GOAL

THIS WEEK'S PRIORITIES	MONDAY	TUESDAY	WEDNESDAY
	TODAY'S GOAL	TODAY'S GOAL	TODAY'S GOAL

	PRIORITIES		PRIORITIES		PRIORITIES
	1		1		1
	2		2		2
	3		3		3
	4am		4am		4am
	5am		5am		5am
	6am		6am		6am
	7am		7am		7am
	8am		8am		8am
	9am		9am		9am
	10am		10am		10am
	11am		11am		11am
	12am		12am		12am
	1pm		1pm		1pm
	2pm		2pm		2pm
	3pm		3pm		3pm
	4pm		4pm		4pm
	5pm		5pm		5pm
	6pm		6pm		6pm
	7pm		7pm		7pm
	9pm		9pm		9pm
	10pm		10pm		10pm

ERRANDS

POSITIVE PATTERNS

	S	M	T	W	T	F	S
PHYSICAL							
PERSONAL							
PROFESSIONAL							

EVOLVING BEAUTY

THE PLANNER
ESSENTIAL TACTICS TO BEING
happy
& SUCCESSFUL

EVOLVING
BEAUTY

THE PLANNER
ESSENTIAL TACTICS TO BEING

happy
& SUCCESSFUL

THURSDAY		FRIDAY		SATURDAY		SUNDAY	
TODAY'S GOAL		TODAY'S GOAL		TODAY'S GOAL		TODAY'S GOAL	
PRIORITIES		PRIORITIES		PRIORITIES		PRIORITIES	
1		1		1		1	
2		2		2		2	
3		3		3		3	
4am		4am		4am		4am	
5am		5am		5am		5am	
6am		6am		6am		6am	
7am		7am		7am		7am	
8am		8am		8am		8am	
9am		9am		9am		9am	
10am		10am		10am		10am	
11am		11am		11am		11am	
12am		12am		12am		12am	
1pm		1pm		1pm		1pm	
2pm		2pm		2pm		2pm	
3pm		3pm		3pm		3pm	
4pm		4pm		4pm		4pm	
5pm		5pm		5pm		5pm	
6pm		6pm		6pm		6pm	
7pm		7pm		7pm		7pm	
9pm		9pm		9pm		9pm	
10pm		10pm		10pm		10pm	

DISTRACTIONS THIS WEEK	BIG IDEAS THIS WEEK

DATE:

EVOLVING BEAUTY

THE PLANNER
ESSENTIAL TACTICS TO BEING
happy
&
SUCCESSFUL

THIS WEEK'S PRIORITIES

MONDAY	TUESDAY	WEDNESDAY
TODAY'S GOAL	TODAY'S GOAL	TODAY'S GOAL

PRIORITIES		PRIORITIES		PRIORITIES	
1		1		1	
2		2		2	
3		3		3	
4am		4am		4am	
5am		5am		5am	
6am		6am		6am	
7am		7am		7am	
8am		8am		8am	
9am		9am		9am	
10am		10am		10am	
11am		11am		11am	
12am		12am		12am	
1pm		1pm		1pm	
2pm		2pm		2pm	
3pm		3pm		3pm	
4pm		4pm		4pm	
5pm		5pm		5pm	
6pm		6pm		6pm	
7pm		7pm		7pm	
9pm		9pm		9pm	
10pm		10pm		10pm	

ERRANDS

POSITIVE PATTERNS

	S	M	T	W	T	F	S
PHYSICAL							
PERSONAL							
PROFESSIONAL							

THURSDAY		FRIDAY		SATURDAY		SUNDAY	
TODAY'S GOAL		TODAY'S GOAL		TODAY'S GOAL		TODAY'S GOAL	
PRIORITIES		PRIORITIES		PRIORITIES		PRIORITIES	
1		1		1		1	
2		2		2		2	
3		3		3		3	
4am		4am		4am		4am	
5am		5am		5am		5am	
6am		6am		6am		6am	
7am		7am		7am		7am	
8am		8am		8am		8am	
9am		9am		9am		9am	
10am		10am		10am		10am	
11am		11am		11am		11am	
12am		12am		12am		12am	
1pm		1pm		1pm		1pm	
2pm		2pm		2pm		2pm	
3pm		3pm		3pm		3pm	
4pm		4pm		4pm		4pm	
5pm		5pm		5pm		5pm	
6pm		6pm		6pm		6pm	
7pm		7pm		7pm		7pm	
9pm		9pm		9pm		9pm	
10pm		10pm		10pm		10pm	

DISTRACTIONS THIS WEEK	BIG IDEAS THIS WEEK

61

DATE:

THIS WEEK'S GOAL

THE PLANNER
ESSENTIAL TACTICS TO BEING
happy
& SUCCESSFUL

THIS WEEK'S PRIORITIES	MONDAY	TUESDAY	WEDNESDAY
	TODAY'S GOAL	TODAY'S GOAL	TODAY'S GOAL

	PRIORITIES	PRIORITIES	PRIORITIES
	1	1	1
	2	2	2
	3	3	3
	4am	4am	4am
	5am	5am	5am
	6am	6am	6am
	7am	7am	7am
	8am	8am	8am
	9am	9am	9am
	10am	10am	10am
	11am	11am	11am
	12am	12am	12am
	1pm	1pm	1pm
	2pm	2pm	2pm
	3pm	3pm	3pm
	4pm	4pm	4pm
	5pm	5pm	5pm
	6pm	6pm	6pm
	7pm	7pm	7pm
	9pm	9pm	9pm
	10pm	10pm	10pm

ERRANDS

POSITIVE PATTERNS

	S	M	T	W	T	F	S
PHYSICAL							
PERSONAL							
PROFESSIONAL							

THE PLANNER
ESSENTIAL TACTICS TO BEING
happy
& SUCCESSFUL

THURSDAY		FRIDAY		SATURDAY		SUNDAY	
TODAY'S GOAL		TODAY'S GOAL		TODAY'S GOAL		TODAY'S GOAL	
PRIORITIES		PRIORITIES		PRIORITIES		PRIORITIES	
1		1		1		1	
2		2		2		2	
3		3		3		3	
4am		4am		4am		4am	
5am		5am		5am		5am	
6am		6am		6am		6am	
7am		7am		7am		7am	
8am		8am		8am		8am	
9am		9am		9am		9am	
10am		10am		10am		10am	
11am		11am		11am		11am	
12am		12am		12am		12am	
1pm		1pm		1pm		1pm	
2pm		2pm		2pm		2pm	
3pm		3pm		3pm		3pm	
4pm		4pm		4pm		4pm	
5pm		5pm		5pm		5pm	
6pm		6pm		6pm		6pm	
7pm		7pm		7pm		7pm	
9pm		9pm		9pm		9pm	
10pm		10pm		10pm		10pm	

DISTRACTIONS THIS WEEK	BIG IDEAS THIS WEEK

MONTHLY REFLECTION

THE PLANNER
ESSENTIAL TACTICS TO BEING
happy & SUCCESSFUL

Visualize, in gratitude, Achieving Your Goals
Use the senses to see, hear, smell,
and touch the experience of what your success will look and feel like.

	MONTHLY GOAL		ACHIEVEMENT
1			
2			
3			

PERSONAL	TIME SPENT	TACTICS FOR IMPROVEMENT
1		
2		
3		
PROFESSIONAL		
1		
2		
3		
PHYSICAL		
1		
2		
3		

1. WHAT DID I LEARN THIS MONTH?
1.
2.
3.
4.
5.

2. DISTRACTIONS AVOID / FEARS TO FORGE THROUGH
1.
2.
3.
4.
5.

3. PEOPLE I LEARNED FROM OR INSPIRED ME?
1.
2.
3.
4.
5.

4. MISSED OPPORTUNITIES THIS MONTH?
1.
2.
3.
4.
5.

5. WHAT ACTIONS CAN I CORRECT FOR NEXT MONTH?
1.
2.
3.
4.
5.

HOW DID I SPENT MY TIME THIS MONTH?
* KEEP BRAND MASTERY PRIORITIES &
PERSONAL STATEMENT TOP OF MIND.
WHAT YOU SAY AND DO SHOULD ALIGN.

PERSONAL
___% Time

PROFESSIONAL
___% Time

PHYSICAL
___% Time

NOTES

NOTES

DESHAWN HATCHER
MASTER MAKEUP ARTIST

EVOLVING
BEAUTY®
EVOLVINGBEAUTY.INFO

"There's Only
ONE
YOU,
Live Your Life!"

FOUNDER & CEO

deshawn
DESHAWNHATCHER**MAKEUP**ARTIST

DESHAWN HATCHER

Has earned the title **MASTER.** As a 17-year seasoned Professional Makeup artist, few can tout her stunning portfolio of work. Hatcher began her makeup career in film. After 20 indie films, she evolved to beauty and fashion makeup. Her roster has oodles of A-listers: Grammy winners, Academy Award nominees, All-Star athletes, dignitaries, Fortune 500 Executives and movie legends. On any given day, DeShawn can be seen beating the faces of the likes of Beyoncé, Tom Cruise, or Annette Benning. She is the personification of Women in Motion. DeShawn is a warm spirit, a candid conversation with a generous heart. Her light shines brightly!

DeShawn's experience inspired her debut book, ***Assisting Rules! The Ultimate Guide to Assisting Makeup Artist and Hairstylist in Beauty, Fashion, and Print.***

The DeShawn Hatcher Brand is a makeup menagerie of services; Independent Master Makeup Artist & Guru, Vlogger, Blogger, Educator, Speaker, and Mentor.

Her repertoire includes red carpet, celebrity, beauty, fashion, editorial, television, film, and print. You'll also find her on the "Beauty Remix Tour," an intensive national workshop for Makeup Professionals.

I AM

PASSIONATE
PROFESSIONAL

+

GIVING

"Understand Your Skills, Presence, and Attitude—That's What People Will Pay For."

My morning routine is...
I get up, make a cappuccino and respond to my social media followers. Then I start my day.

My business is distinct because...
I work to integrate my business 360.° I seek alternative methods to educate with the Beauty Remix Tour, an intensive 9-hour instructional workshop. I run a tight ship; the instruction is rigorous. I design the workshop this way because I want my students to learn to be their best. The workshop is for Professional Makeup Artist only; I want my students to speed up their makeup application time, develop new skills and no-fail techniques. The course is to get students "un-stuck" out of makeup methods that no longer serve them or the industry.

If I could tell my younger self something about being an entrepreneur... Don't worry, you will be fine, once you follow YOUR dreams. Relax and save your money.

In the future, the beauty industry will...
The future of beauty will include more digital learning tools. I envision Webinar and YouTube 3.0. Also, the makeup color options must have wider ranges, especially for women of color. If big brands don't develop more options women of color, beauty savvy consumers will luxury or prestige brands for their heritage brand name's sake. The emerging independent brands have a huge opportunity.

© EvolvingBeauty.Info

DeShawn is a native New Yorker. She graduated from NYC Beauty School that was film and television focused. She lives in New York City. For more information go to DeShawnHatcher.com | @DeShawnHatcher

EVOLVING BEAUTY

THE PLANNER
ESSENTIAL TACTICS TO BEING
happy
& SUCCESSFUL

MONTH:

MY PERSONAL STATEMENT FOR THE YEAR

"If It were easy, everyone would do it." --PT

SUNDAY	MONDAY	TUESDAY	WEDNESDAY	THURSDAY	FRIDAY	SATURDAY

GRATITUDES/NOTES

Visualize the completion of your Personal, Professional and Physical goals.
Your monthly goals should align with your Brand Mastery Priorities from Step 1.

My Personal Intention is...
1
2
3

My Professional Intention is...
1
2
3

My Physical Intention is...
1
2
3

DATE:

THIS WEEK'S GOAL

THIS WEEK'S PRIORITIES

MONDAY	TUESDAY	WEDNESDAY
TODAY'S GOAL	TODAY'S GOAL	TODAY'S GOAL
PRIORITIES	PRIORITIES	PRIORITIES
1	1	1
2	2	2
3	3	3
4am	4am	4am
5am	5am	5am
6am	6am	6am
7am	7am	7am
8am	8am	8am
9am	9am	9am
10am	10am	10am
11am	11am	11am
12am	12am	12am
1pm	1pm	1pm
2pm	2pm	2pm
3pm	3pm	3pm
4pm	4pm	4pm
5pm	5pm	5pm
6pm	6pm	6pm
7pm	7pm	7pm
9pm	9pm	9pm
10pm	10pm	10pm

ERRANDS

POSITIVE PATTERNS	S	M	T	W	T	F	S
PHYSICAL							
PERSONAL							
PROFESSIONAL							

70

THE PLANNER

ESSENTIAL TACTICS TO BEING

happy
& SUCCESSFUL

THURSDAY		FRIDAY		SATURDAY		SUNDAY	
TODAY'S GOAL		TODAY'S GOAL		TODAY'S GOAL		TODAY'S GOAL	
PRIORITIES		PRIORITIES		PRIORITIES		PRIORITIES	
1		1		1		1	
2		2		2		2	
3		3		3		3	
4am		4am		4am		4am	
5am		5am		5am		5am	
6am		6am		6am		6am	
7am		7am		7am		7am	
8am		8am		8am		8am	
9am		9am		9am		9am	
10am		10am		10am		10am	
11am		11am		11am		11am	
12am		12am		12am		12am	
1pm		1pm		1pm		1pm	
2pm		2pm		2pm		2pm	
3pm		3pm		3pm		3pm	
4pm		4pm		4pm		4pm	
5pm		5pm		5pm		5pm	
6pm		6pm		6pm		6pm	
7pm		7pm		7pm		7pm	
9pm		9pm		9pm		9pm	
10pm		10pm		10pm		10pm	

DISTRACTIONS THIS WEEK	BIG IDEAS THIS WEEK

DATE:

THIS WEEK'S GOAL

EVOLVING BEAUTY

THE PLANNER
ESSENTIAL TACTICS TO BEING
happy
& SUCCESSFUL

THIS WEEK'S PRIORITIES	MONDAY	TUESDAY	WEDNESDAY
	TODAY'S GOAL	TODAY'S GOAL	TODAY'S GOAL
	PRIORITIES	PRIORITIES	PRIORITIES
	1	1	1
	2	2	2
	3	3	3
	4am	4am	4am
	5am	5am	5am
	6am	6am	6am
	7am	7am	7am
	8am	8am	8am
	9am	9am	9am
	10am	10am	10am
	11am	11am	11am
	12am	12am	12am
	1pm	1pm	1pm
	2pm	2pm	2pm
	3pm	3pm	3pm
	4pm	4pm	4pm
	5pm	5pm	5pm
	6pm	6pm	6pm
	7pm	7pm	7pm
	9pm	9pm	9pm
	10pm	10pm	10pm

ERRANDS

POSITIVE PATTERNS

	S	M	T	W	T	F	S
PHYSICAL							
PERSONAL							
PROFESSIONAL							

THURSDAY		FRIDAY		SATURDAY		SUNDAY	
TODAY'S GOAL		TODAY'S GOAL		TODAY'S GOAL		TODAY'S GOAL	
PRIORITIES		PRIORITIES		PRIORITIES		PRIORITIES	
1		1		1		1	
2		2		2		2	
3		3		3		3	
4am		4am		4am		4am	
5am		5am		5am		5am	
6am		6am		6am		6am	
7am		7am		7am		7am	
8am		8am		8am		8am	
9am		9am		9am		9am	
10am		10am		10am		10am	
11am		11am		11am		11am	
12am		12am		12am		12am	
1pm		1pm		1pm		1pm	
2pm		2pm		2pm		2pm	
3pm		3pm		3pm		3pm	
4pm		4pm		4pm		4pm	
5pm		5pm		5pm		5pm	
6pm		6pm		6pm		6pm	
7pm		7pm		7pm		7pm	
9pm		9pm		9pm		9pm	
10pm		10pm		10pm		10pm	

DISTRACTIONS THIS WEEK	BIG IDEAS THIS WEEK

DATE:

THIS WEEK'S GOAL

EVOLVING BEAUTY

THE PLANNER
ESSENTIAL TACTICS TO BEING
happy
& SUCCESSFUL

THIS WEEK'S PRIORITIES

MONDAY	TUESDAY	WEDNESDAY
TODAY'S GOAL	TODAY'S GOAL	TODAY'S GOAL

PRIORITIES	PRIORITIES	PRIORITIES
1	1	1
2	2	2
3	3	3
4am	4am	4am
5am	5am	5am
6am	6am	6am
7am	7am	7am
8am	8am	8am
9am	9am	9am
10am	10am	10am
11am	11am	11am
12am	12am	12am
1pm	1pm	1pm
2pm	2pm	2pm
3pm	3pm	3pm
4pm	4pm	4pm
5pm	5pm	5pm
6pm	6pm	6pm
7pm	7pm	7pm
9pm	9pm	9pm
10pm	10pm	10pm

ERRANDS

POSITIVE PATTERNS

	S	M	T	W	T	F	S
PHYSICAL							
PERSONAL							
PROFESSIONAL							

74

THE PLANNER

ESSENTIAL TACTICS TO BEING

happy
& SUCCESSFUL

THURSDAY		FRIDAY		SATURDAY		SUNDAY	
TODAY'S GOAL		TODAY'S GOAL		TODAY'S GOAL		TODAY'S GOAL	
PRIORITIES		PRIORITIES		PRIORITIES		PRIORITIES	
1		1		1		1	
2		2		2		2	
3		3		3		3	
4am		4am		4am		4am	
5am		5am		5am		5am	
6am		6am		6am		6am	
7am		7am		7am		7am	
8am		8am		8am		8am	
9am		9am		9am		9am	
10am		10am		10am		10am	
11am		11am		11am		11am	
12am		12am		12am		12am	
1pm		1pm		1pm		1pm	
2pm		2pm		2pm		2pm	
3pm		3pm		3pm		3pm	
4pm		4pm		4pm		4pm	
5pm		5pm		5pm		5pm	
6pm		6pm		6pm		6pm	
7pm		7pm		7pm		7pm	
9pm		9pm		9pm		9pm	
10pm		10pm		10pm		10pm	

DISTRACTIONS THIS WEEK	BIG IDEAS THIS WEEK

DATE:

THIS WEEK'S GOAL

EVOLVING BEAUTY

THE PLANNER
ESSENTIAL TACTICS TO BEING
happy
& SUCCESSFUL

THIS WEEK'S PRIORITIES	MONDAY		TUESDAY		WEDNESDAY	
	TODAY'S GOAL		TODAY'S GOAL		TODAY'S GOAL	
	PRIORITIES		PRIORITIES		PRIORITIES	
	1		1		1	
	2		2		2	
	3		3		3	
	4am		4am		4am	
	5am		5am		5am	
	6am		6am		6am	
	7am		7am		7am	
	8am		8am		8am	
	9am		9am		9am	
	10am		10am		10am	
	11am		11am		11am	
	12am		12am		12am	
	1pm		1pm		1pm	
	2pm		2pm		2pm	
	3pm		3pm		3pm	
	4pm		4pm		4pm	
	5pm		5pm		5pm	
	6pm		6pm		6pm	
	7pm		7pm		7pm	
	9pm		9pm		9pm	
	10pm		10pm		10pm	

ERRANDS

POSITIVE PATTERNS	S	M	T	W	T	F	S
PHYSICAL							
PERSONAL							
PROFESSIONAL							

THE PLANNER

ESSENTIAL TACTICS TO BEING

happy

& SUCCESSFUL

THURSDAY		FRIDAY		SATURDAY		SUNDAY	
TODAY'S GOAL		TODAY'S GOAL		TODAY'S GOAL		TODAY'S GOAL	
PRIORITIES		PRIORITIES		PRIORITIES		PRIORITIES	
1		1		1		1	
2		2		2		2	
3		3		3		3	
4am		4am		4am		4am	
5am		5am		5am		5am	
6am		6am		6am		6am	
7am		7am		7am		7am	
8am		8am		8am		8am	
9am		9am		9am		9am	
10am		10am		10am		10am	
11am		11am		11am		11am	
12am		12am		12am		12am	
1pm		1pm		1pm		1pm	
2pm		2pm		2pm		2pm	
3pm		3pm		3pm		3pm	
4pm		4pm		4pm		4pm	
5pm		5pm		5pm		5pm	
6pm		6pm		6pm		6pm	
7pm		7pm		7pm		7pm	
9pm		9pm		9pm		9pm	
10pm		10pm		10pm		10pm	

DISTRACTIONS THIS WEEK	BIG IDEAS THIS WEEK

DATE:

THIS WEEK'S GOAL

EVOLVING
BEAUTY

THE PLANNER
ESSENTIAL TACTICS TO BEING
happy
& SUCCESSFUL

THIS WEEK'S PRIORITIES	MONDAY	TUESDAY	WEDNESDAY
	TODAY'S GOAL	TODAY'S GOAL	TODAY'S GOAL

	PRIORITIES	PRIORITIES	PRIORITIES
	1	1	1
	2	2	2
	3	3	3
	4am	4am	4am
	5am	5am	5am
	6am	6am	6am
	7am	7am	7am
	8am	8am	8am
	9am	9am	9am
	10am	10am	10am
	11am	11am	11am
	12am	12am	12am
	1pm	1pm	1pm
	2pm	2pm	2pm
	3pm	3pm	3pm
	4pm	4pm	4pm
	5pm	5pm	5pm
	6pm	6pm	6pm
	7pm	7pm	7pm
	9pm	9pm	9pm
	10pm	10pm	10pm

ERRANDS

POSITIVE PATTERNS

	S	M	T	W	T	F	S
PHYSICAL							
PERSONAL							
PROFESSIONAL							

THURSDAY		FRIDAY		SATURDAY		SUNDAY	
TODAY'S GOAL		TODAY'S GOAL		TODAY'S GOAL		TODAY'S GOAL	
PRIORITIES		PRIORITIES		PRIORITIES		PRIORITIES	
1		1		1		1	
2		2		2		2	
3		3		3		3	
4am		4am		4am		4am	
5am		5am		5am		5am	
6am		6am		6am		6am	
7am		7am		7am		7am	
8am		8am		8am		8am	
9am		9am		9am		9am	
10am		10am		10am		10am	
11am		11am		11am		11am	
12am		12am		12am		12am	
1pm		1pm		1pm		1pm	
2pm		2pm		2pm		2pm	
3pm		3pm		3pm		3pm	
4pm		4pm		4pm		4pm	
5pm		5pm		5pm		5pm	
6pm		6pm		6pm		6pm	
7pm		7pm		7pm		7pm	
9pm		9pm		9pm		9pm	
10pm		10pm		10pm		10pm	

DISTRACTIONS THIS WEEK	BIG IDEAS THIS WEEK

MONTHLY REFLECTION

Visualize, in gratitude, Achieving Your Goals
*Use the senses to see, hear, smell,
and touch the experience of what your success will look and feel like.*

	MONTHLY GOAL		ACHIEVEMENT
1			
2			
3			

	PERSONAL	TIME SPENT	TACTICS FOR IMPROVEMENT
1			
2			
3			
	PROFESSIONAL		
1			
2			
3			
	PHYSICAL		
1			
2			
3			

1. WHAT DID I LEARN THIS MONTH?
1.
2.
3.
4.
5.

2. DISTRACTIONS AVOID / FEARS TO FORGE THROUGH
1.
2.
3.
4.
5.

3. PEOPLE I LEARNED FROM OR INSPIRED ME?
1.
2.
3.
4.
5.

4. MISSED OPPORTUNITIES THIS MONTH?
1.
2.
3.
4.
5.

5. WHAT ACTIONS CAN I CORRECT FOR NEXT MONTH?
1.
2.
3.
4.
5.

HOW DID I SPENT MY TIME THIS MONTH?
* KEEP BRAND MASTERY PRIORITIES &
PERSONAL STATEMENT TOP OF MIND.
WHAT YOU SAY AND DO SHOULD ALIGN.

PERSONAL
___% Time

PROFESSIONAL
___% Time

PHYSICAL
___% Time

NOTES

NOTES

CARLINE DARGENSON
THE HAIR ARTIST

"Business is Never Personal."

FOUNDER & MASTER STYLIST

CARLINE DARGENSON

Has an affinity for hair; professionalism, education, and artistry are her forte.
Carline's love of art began as a young girl drawing and sketching.
Her passion for sketching evolved into her love of creating art with shears. As a second generation Beauty Professional she enjoys the freedom of being an independent Master Stylist & Educator. **THE HAIR ARTIST.**

My morning routine is...
I wake up, have coffee and take my daughter to school. When I return home, I start my day. I work out 3x's a week. Working out is important for overall good health. But, as a stylist we are on our feet every day, it's vital to have a strong core.

I started in the beauty industry by...
I'm a 2nd generation Beauty Professional. I grew up in my Mom's Hair Salon/Beauty Supply store. I had pristine finger waves and curly-cued Jheri curls. I became familiar with all types of beauty products at an early age.

I was a psychology major in college. I never intended to be a stylist. I entered hair school part-time and fell in love with it. I've been an educator for Vidal Sasson,Mizani/L'Oreal, and Next Level Concepts with Denise Michelle. I'm an advocate of continuing education courses whenever possible. There is always more to learn. I love teaching and learning.

I love the beauty industry because...
I love the freedom it gives. What you put in, you get out. I love making people beautiful.

My business mantra...
Business is Never Personal!

Carline is the face of InStylHairCare. She has been a stylist for over 15 years. She loves to teach her clients how to properly care and maintain their hair.

"No Negativity Allowed"

INSTYL
HAIRCARE
HAIR EDUCATOR
ARTIST
+ MASTER STYLIST

I AM HUMOROUS. **+** TO-THE-POINT. WITH A BIG ♥

Carline has a thriving beauty business as a hair stylist in NYC.
She resides in Brooklyn, NY.
For more information go to
InStylHairCare.com | @InStylHairCare

EVOLVING BEAUTY
© EvolvingBeauty.Info

MONTH:

MY PERSONAL STATEMENT FOR THE YEAR

"I am not free when any woman is unfree, even if her shackles are very different from my own." ~Audrey Lourde:

EVOLVING
BEAUTY

THE PLANNER
ESSENTIAL TACTICS TO BEING
happy
& SUCCESSFUL

SUNDAY	MONDAY	TUESDAY	WEDNESDAY	THURSDAY	FRIDAY	SATURDAY

Visualize the completion of your Personal, Professional and Physical goals.
*Your monthly goals should align with your **Brand Mastery Priorities** from Step 1.*

My Personal Intention is...
1
2
3

My Professional Intention is...
1
2
3

My Physical Intention is...
1
2
3

GRATITUDES/NOTES

DATE:

EVOLVING BEAUTY
THE PLANNER
ESSENTIAL TACTICS TO BEING
happy
& SUCCESSFUL

THIS WEEK'S PRIORITIES	MONDAY	TUESDAY	WEDNESDAY
	TODAY'S GOAL	TODAY'S GOAL	TODAY'S GOAL
	PRIORITIES	PRIORITIES	PRIORITIES
	1	1	1
	2	2	2
	3	3	3
	4am	4am	4am
	5am	5am	5am
	6am	6am	6am
	7am	7am	7am
	8am	8am	8am
	9am	9am	9am
	10am	10am	10am
	11am	11am	11am
	12am	12am	12am
	1pm	1pm	1pm
	2pm	2pm	2pm
	3pm	3pm	3pm
	4pm	4pm	4pm
	5pm	5pm	5pm
	6pm	6pm	6pm
	7pm	7pm	7pm
	9pm	9pm	9pm
	10pm	10pm	10pm

ERRANDS

POSITIVE PATTERNS	S	M	T	W	T	F	S
PHYSICAL							
PERSONAL							
PROFESSIONAL							

THURSDAY		FRIDAY		SATURDAY		SUNDAY	
TODAY'S GOAL		TODAY'S GOAL		TODAY'S GOAL		TODAY'S GOAL	
PRIORITIES		PRIORITIES		PRIORITIES		PRIORITIES	
1		1		1		1	
2		2		2		2	
3		3		3		3	
4am		4am		4am		4am	
5am		5am		5am		5am	
6am		6am		6am		6am	
7am		7am		7am		7am	
8am		8am		8am		8am	
9am		9am		9am		9am	
10am		10am		10am		10am	
11am		11am		11am		11am	
12am		12am		12am		12am	
1pm		1pm		1pm		1pm	
2pm		2pm		2pm		2pm	
3pm		3pm		3pm		3pm	
4pm		4pm		4pm		4pm	
5pm		5pm		5pm		5pm	
6pm		6pm		6pm		6pm	
7pm		7pm		7pm		7pm	
9pm		9pm		9pm		9pm	
10pm		10pm		10pm		10pm	

DISTRACTIONS THIS WEEK	BIG IDEAS THIS WEEK

DATE:

THIS WEEK'S GOAL

EVOLVING BEAUTY

THE PLANNER
ESSENTIAL TACTICS TO BEING
happy
& SUCCESSFUL

THIS WEEK'S PRIORITIES	MONDAY	TUESDAY	WEDNESDAY
	TODAY'S GOAL	TODAY'S GOAL	TODAY'S GOAL
	PRIORITIES	PRIORITIES	PRIORITIES
	1	1	1
	2	2	2
	3	3	3
	4am	4am	4am
	5am	5am	5am
	6am	6am	6am
	7am	7am	7am
	8am	8am	8am
	9am	9am	9am
	10am	10am	10am
	11am	11am	11am
	12am	12am	12am
	1pm	1pm	1pm
	2pm	2pm	2pm
	3pm	3pm	3pm
	4pm	4pm	4pm
	5pm	5pm	5pm
	6pm	6pm	6pm
	7pm	7pm	7pm
	9pm	9pm	9pm
	10pm	10pm	10pm

ERRANDS

POSITIVE PATTERNS							
	S	M	T	W	T	F	S
PHYSICAL							
PERSONAL							
PROFESSIONAL							

THURSDAY		FRIDAY		SATURDAY		SUNDAY	
TODAY'S GOAL		TODAY'S GOAL		TODAY'S GOAL		TODAY'S GOAL	
PRIORITIES		PRIORITIES		PRIORITIES		PRIORITIES	
1		1		1		1	
2		2		2		2	
3		3		3		3	
4am		4am		4am		4am	
5am		5am		5am		5am	
6am		6am		6am		6am	
7am		7am		7am		7am	
8am		8am		8am		8am	
9am		9am		9am		9am	
10am		10am		10am		10am	
11am		11am		11am		11am	
12am		12am		12am		12am	
1pm		1pm		1pm		1pm	
2pm		2pm		2pm		2pm	
3pm		3pm		3pm		3pm	
4pm		4pm		4pm		4pm	
5pm		5pm		5pm		5pm	
6pm		6pm		6pm		6pm	
7pm		7pm		7pm		7pm	
9pm		9pm		9pm		9pm	
10pm		10pm		10pm		10pm	

DISTRACTIONS THIS WEEK	BIG IDEAS THIS WEEK

DATE:

THE PLANNER
ESSENTIAL TACTICS TO BEING
happy
& SUCCESSFUL

THIS WEEK'S GOAL

THIS WEEK'S PRIORITIES	MONDAY	TUESDAY	WEDNESDAY
	TODAY'S GOAL	TODAY'S GOAL	TODAY'S GOAL
	PRIORITIES	PRIORITIES	PRIORITIES
	1	1	1
	2	2	2
	3	3	3
	4am	4am	4am
	5am	5am	5am
	6am	6am	6am
	7am	7am	7am
	8am	8am	8am
	9am	9am	9am
	10am	10am	10am
	11am	11am	11am
	12am	12am	12am
	1pm	1pm	1pm
	2pm	2pm	2pm
	3pm	3pm	3pm
	4pm	4pm	4pm
	5pm	5pm	5pm
	6pm	6pm	6pm
	7pm	7pm	7pm
	9pm	9pm	9pm
	10pm	10pm	10pm

ERRANDS

POSITIVE PATTERNS

	S	M	T	W	T	F	S
PHYSICAL							
PERSONAL							
PROFESSIONAL							

THE PLANNER
ESSENTIAL TACTICS TO BEING
happy
& SUCCESSFUL

THURSDAY		FRIDAY		SATURDAY		SUNDAY	
TODAY'S GOAL		TODAY'S GOAL		TODAY'S GOAL		TODAY'S GOAL	
PRIORITIES		PRIORITIES		PRIORITIES		PRIORITIES	
1		1		1		1	
2		2		2		2	
3		3		3		3	
4am		4am		4am		4am	
5am		5am		5am		5am	
6am		6am		6am		6am	
7am		7am		7am		7am	
8am		8am		8am		8am	
9am		9am		9am		9am	
10am		10am		10am		10am	
11am		11am		11am		11am	
12am		12am		12am		12am	
1pm		1pm		1pm		1pm	
2pm		2pm		2pm		2pm	
3pm		3pm		3pm		3pm	
4pm		4pm		4pm		4pm	
5pm		5pm		5pm		5pm	
6pm		6pm		6pm		6pm	
7pm		7pm		7pm		7pm	
9pm		9pm		9pm		9pm	
10pm		10pm		10pm		10pm	

DISTRACTIONS THIS WEEK	BIG IDEAS THIS WEEK

DATE:

THIS WEEK'S GOAL

EVOLVING BEAUTY

THE PLANNER
ESSENTIAL TACTICS TO BEING
happy
& SUCCESSFUL

THIS WEEK'S PRIORITIES	MONDAY	TUESDAY	WEDNESDAY
	TODAY'S GOAL	TODAY'S GOAL	TODAY'S GOAL
	PRIORITIES	PRIORITIES	PRIORITIES
	1	1	1
	2	2	2
	3	3	3
	4am	4am	4am
	5am	5am	5am
	6am	6am	6am
	7am	7am	7am
	8am	8am	8am
	9am	9am	9am
	10am	10am	10am
	11am	11am	11am
	12am	12am	12am
	1pm	1pm	1pm
	2pm	2pm	2pm
	3pm	3pm	3pm
	4pm	4pm	4pm
	5pm	5pm	5pm
	6pm	6pm	6pm
	7pm	7pm	7pm
	9pm	9pm	9pm
	10pm	10pm	10pm

ERRANDS

POSITIVE PATTERNS

	S	M	T	W	T	F	S
PHYSICAL							
PERSONAL							
PROFESSIONAL							

THE PLANNER
ESSENTIAL TACTICS TO BEING
happy
& SUCCESSFUL

THURSDAY		FRIDAY		SATURDAY		SUNDAY	
TODAY'S GOAL		TODAY'S GOAL		TODAY'S GOAL		TODAY'S GOAL	
PRIORITIES		PRIORITIES		PRIORITIES		PRIORITIES	
1		1		1		1	
2		2		2		2	
3		3		3		3	
4am		4am		4am		4am	
5am		5am		5am		5am	
6am		6am		6am		6am	
7am		7am		7am		7am	
8am		8am		8am		8am	
9am		9am		9am		9am	
10am		10am		10am		10am	
11am		11am		11am		11am	
12am		12am		12am		12am	
1pm		1pm		1pm		1pm	
2pm		2pm		2pm		2pm	
3pm		3pm		3pm		3pm	
4pm		4pm		4pm		4pm	
5pm		5pm		5pm		5pm	
6pm		6pm		6pm		6pm	
7pm		7pm		7pm		7pm	
9pm		9pm		9pm		9pm	
10pm		10pm		10pm		10pm	

DISTRACTIONS THIS WEEK	BIG IDEAS THIS WEEK

DATE:

THIS WEEK'S GOAL

EVOLVING
BEAUTY

THE PLANNER
ESSENTIAL TACTICS TO BEING
happy
& SUCCESSFUL

THIS WEEK'S PRIORITIES	MONDAY		TUESDAY		WEDNESDAY	
	TODAY'S GOAL		TODAY'S GOAL		TODAY'S GOAL	
	PRIORITIES		PRIORITIES		PRIORITIES	
	1		1		1	
	2		2		2	
	3		3		3	
	4am		4am		4am	
	5am		5am		5am	
	6am		6am		6am	
	7am		7am		7am	
	8am		8am		8am	
	9am		9am		9am	
	10am		10am		10am	
	11am		11am		11am	
	12am		12am		12am	
	1pm		1pm		1pm	
	2pm		2pm		2pm	
	3pm		3pm		3pm	
	4pm		4pm		4pm	
	5pm		5pm		5pm	
	6pm		6pm		6pm	
	7pm		7pm		7pm	
	9pm		9pm		9pm	
	10pm		10pm		10pm	

ERRANDS	POSITIVE PATTERNS						
		S	M	T	W	T	F	S
	PHYSICAL							
	PERSONAL							
	PROFESSIONAL							

THURSDAY		FRIDAY		SATURDAY		SUNDAY	
TODAY'S GOAL		TODAY'S GOAL		TODAY'S GOAL		TODAY'S GOAL	
PRIORITIES		**PRIORITIES**		**PRIORITIES**		**PRIORITIES**	
1		1		1		1	
2		2		2		2	
3		3		3		3	
4am		4am		4am		4am	
5am		5am		5am		5am	
6am		6am		6am		6am	
7am		7am		7am		7am	
8am		8am		8am		8am	
9am		9am		9am		9am	
10am		10am		10am		10am	
11am		11am		11am		11am	
12am		12am		12am		12am	
1pm		1pm		1pm		1pm	
2pm		2pm		2pm		2pm	
3pm		3pm		3pm		3pm	
4pm		4pm		4pm		4pm	
5pm		5pm		5pm		5pm	
6pm		6pm		6pm		6pm	
7pm		7pm		7pm		7pm	
9pm		9pm		9pm		9pm	
10pm		10pm		10pm		10pm	

DISTRACTIONS THIS WEEK	BIG IDEAS THIS WEEK

MONTHLY REFLECTION

Visualize, in gratitude, Achieving Your Goals
Use the senses to see, hear, smell,
and touch the experience of what your success will look and feel like.

	MONTHLY GOAL		ACHIEVEMENT
1			
2			
3			

	PERSONAL	TIME SPENT	TACTICS FOR IMPROVEMENT
1			
2			
3			
	PROFESSIONAL		
1			
2			
3			
	PHYSICAL		
1			
2			
3			

1. WHAT DID I LEARN THIS MONTH?
1.
2.
3.
4.
5.

2. DISTRACTIONS AVOID / FEARS TO FORGE THROUGH
1.
2.
3.
4.
5.

3. PEOPLE I LEARNED FROM OR INSPIRED ME?
1.
2.
3.
4.
5.

4. MISSED OPPORTUNITIES THIS MONTH?
1.
2.
3.
4.
5.

5. WHAT ACTIONS CAN I CORRECT FOR NEXT MONTH?
1.
2.
3.
4.
5.

HOW DID I SPENT MY TIME THIS MONTH?
* KEEP BRAND MASTERY PRIORITIES &
PERSONAL STATEMENT TOP OF MIND.
WHAT YOU SAY AND DO SHOULD ALIGN.

PERSONAL
___% Time

PROFESSIONAL
___% Time

PHYSICAL
___% Time

NOTES

RACHEL ODEM
THE TRIPLE THREAT

"*You can do anything you put your mind to, and work for.*"

NATURAL VLOGGER
SKIN CARE THERAPIST
MAKEUP ARTIST
CEO
INFLUENCER

Rachel O.

BEAUTY

RACHEL ODEM

Is a Licensed Skincare Therapist, Makeup Artist and Naturalista of over 15 years. Rachel O Beauty is the **TRIPLE THREAT OF BEAUTY INFLUENCERS**, the "go-to" for Vlogger/Blogger brand awareness. In 2016 Natural Meet-Up Chicago, founded by Rachel O Beauty in 2010, was ranked one of the largest in the U.S.* Her beauty acumen is infectious, she's personable, knowledgeable and honest.

"Your Business Will Stop Growing, When You Stop Talking About It."

My morning routine is...
Prayer, positive worship/music, social media management and preparing my family for the day.

I started my own business because...
I wanted to work for myself from home so I could be a stay-at-home Mom to my three (3) daughters.

I love the beauty industry because...
It is alive, with creativity and artistry.

How has the Digital Age changed your business?
It has opened doors to work with some of my favorite brands and to become a well known beauty expert. Although, social media can be very distracting. Sometimes I have a love/hate relationship with the internet.

My business mantra...
ABC – Always Be Creating!

She's a Vlogger/Blogger Extraordinaire. Additional services include brand awareness for beauty and lifestyle brands; Campaign Brand Ambassador, Host, Model Spokesperson, Social Media Consultation and Other Program Partnerships.

I AM
CREATIVE
SELF
MOTIVATING
+ GIVING

Rachel is a native of Chicago, IL, where she currently resides with her family. She is a Licensed Skincare Therapist and Makeup Artist. For more information go to RachelOBeauty.com | @RachelOBeauty

NaturalHair.MeetUup.com

MY PERSONAL STATEMENT FOR THE YEAR

MONTH:

"You can't keep covering up the trash, sometimes you have to take it out." –Deja Bell

SUNDAY	MONDAY	TUESDAY	WEDNESDAY	THURSDAY	FRIDAY	SATURDAY

GRATITUDES/NOTES

Visualize the completion of your Personal, Professional and Physical goals.
*Your monthly goals should align with your **Brand Mastery Priorities** from Step 1.*

My Personal Intention is...
1
2
3

My Professional Intention is...
1
2
3

My Physical Intention is...
1
2
3

DATE:

THIS WEEK'S GOAL

THIS WEEK'S PRIORITIES	MONDAY	TUESDAY	WEDNESDAY
	TODAY'S GOAL	TODAY'S GOAL	TODAY'S GOAL
	PRIORITIES	PRIORITIES	PRIORITIES
	1	1	1
	2	2	2
	3	3	3
	4am	4am	4am
	5am	5am	5am
	6am	6am	6am
	7am	7am	7am
	8am	8am	8am
	9am	9am	9am
	10am	10am	10am
	11am	11am	11am
	12am	12am	12am
	1pm	1pm	1pm
	2pm	2pm	2pm
	3pm	3pm	3pm
	4pm	4pm	4pm
	5pm	5pm	5pm
	6pm	6pm	6pm
	7pm	7pm	7pm
	9pm	9pm	9pm
	10pm	10pm	10pm

ERRANDS	POSITIVE PATTERNS						
		S	M	T	W	T	F	S
	PHYSICAL						
	PERSONAL						
	PROFESSIONAL						

THE PLANNER
ESSENTIAL TACTICS TO BEING
happy
& SUCCESSFUL

THURSDAY		FRIDAY		SATURDAY		SUNDAY	
TODAY'S GOAL		TODAY'S GOAL		TODAY'S GOAL		TODAY'S GOAL	
PRIORITIES		PRIORITIES		PRIORITIES		PRIORITIES	
1		1		1		1	
2		2		2		2	
3		3		3		3	
4am		4am		4am		4am	
5am		5am		5am		5am	
6am		6am		6am		6am	
7am		7am		7am		7am	
8am		8am		8am		8am	
9am		9am		9am		9am	
10am		10am		10am		10am	
11am		11am		11am		11am	
12am		12am		12am		12am	
1pm		1pm		1pm		1pm	
2pm		2pm		2pm		2pm	
3pm		3pm		3pm		3pm	
4pm		4pm		4pm		4pm	
5pm		5pm		5pm		5pm	
6pm		6pm		6pm		6pm	
7pm		7pm		7pm		7pm	
9pm		9pm		9pm		9pm	
10pm		10pm		10pm		10pm	

DISTRACTIONS THIS WEEK	BIG IDEAS THIS WEEK

DATE:

THIS WEEK'S GOAL

THIS WEEK'S PRIORITIES	MONDAY	TUESDAY	WEDNESDAY
	TODAY'S GOAL	TODAY'S GOAL	TODAY'S GOAL

	PRIORITIES	PRIORITIES	PRIORITIES
	1	1	1
	2	2	2
	3	3	3
	4am	4am	4am
	5am	5am	5am
	6am	6am	6am
	7am	7am	7am
	8am	8am	8am
	9am	9am	9am
	10am	10am	10am
	11am	11am	11am
	12am	12am	12am
	1pm	1pm	1pm
	2pm	2pm	2pm
	3pm	3pm	3pm
	4pm	4pm	4pm
	5pm	5pm	5pm
	6pm	6pm	6pm
	7pm	7pm	7pm
	9pm	9pm	9pm
	10pm	10pm	10pm

ERRANDS

POSITIVE PATTERNS

	S	M	T	W	T	F	S
PHYSICAL							
PERSONAL							
PROFESSIONAL							

THURSDAY		FRIDAY		SATURDAY		SUNDAY	
TODAY'S GOAL		TODAY'S GOAL		TODAY'S GOAL		TODAY'S GOAL	
PRIORITIES		PRIORITIES		PRIORITIES		PRIORITIES	
1		1		1		1	
2		2		2		2	
3		3		3		3	
4am		4am		4am		4am	
5am		5am		5am		5am	
6am		6am		6am		6am	
7am		7am		7am		7am	
8am		8am		8am		8am	
9am		9am		9am		9am	
10am		10am		10am		10am	
11am		11am		11am		11am	
12am		12am		12am		12am	
1pm		1pm		1pm		1pm	
2pm		2pm		2pm		2pm	
3pm		3pm		3pm		3pm	
4pm		4pm		4pm		4pm	
5pm		5pm		5pm		5pm	
6pm		6pm		6pm		6pm	
7pm		7pm		7pm		7pm	
9pm		9pm		9pm		9pm	
10pm		10pm		10pm		10pm	

DISTRACTIONS THIS WEEK	BIG IDEAS THIS WEEK

DATE:

THE PLANNER
ESSENTIAL TACTICS TO BEING
happy
& SUCCESSFUL

THIS WEEK'S PRIORITIES	MONDAY	TUESDAY	WEDNESDAY
	TODAY'S GOAL	TODAY'S GOAL	TODAY'S GOAL
	PRIORITIES	PRIORITIES	PRIORITIES
	1	1	1
	2	2	2
	3	3	3
	4am	4am	4am
	5am	5am	5am
	6am	6am	6am
	7am	7am	7am
	8am	8am	8am
	9am	9am	9am
	10am	10am	10am
	11am	11am	11am
	12am	12am	12am
	1pm	1pm	1pm
	2pm	2pm	2pm
	3pm	3pm	3pm
	4pm	4pm	4pm
	5pm	5pm	5pm
	6pm	6pm	6pm
	7pm	7pm	7pm
	9pm	9pm	9pm
	10pm	10pm	10pm

ERRANDS

POSITIVE PATTERNS	S	M	T	W	T	F	S
PHYSICAL							
PERSONAL							
PROFESSIONAL							

THE PLANNER
ESSENTIAL TACTICS TO BEING
happy
& SUCCESSFUL

THURSDAY		FRIDAY		SATURDAY		SUNDAY	
TODAY'S GOAL		TODAY'S GOAL		TODAY'S GOAL		TODAY'S GOAL	
PRIORITIES		PRIORITIES		PRIORITIES		PRIORITIES	
1		1		1		1	
2		2		2		2	
3		3		3		3	
4am		4am		4am		4am	
5am		5am		5am		5am	
6am		6am		6am		6am	
7am		7am		7am		7am	
8am		8am		8am		8am	
9am		9am		9am		9am	
10am		10am		10am		10am	
11am		11am		11am		11am	
12am		12am		12am		12am	
1pm		1pm		1pm		1pm	
2pm		2pm		2pm		2pm	
3pm		3pm		3pm		3pm	
4pm		4pm		4pm		4pm	
5pm		5pm		5pm		5pm	
6pm		6pm		6pm		6pm	
7pm		7pm		7pm		7pm	
9pm		9pm		9pm		9pm	
10pm		10pm		10pm		10pm	

DISTRACTIONS THIS WEEK	BIG IDEAS THIS WEEK

DATE:

THIS WEEK'S GOAL

EVOLVING BEAUTY

THE PLANNER
ESSENTIAL TACTICS TO BEING
happy
&
SUCCESSFUL

THIS WEEK'S PRIORITIES	MONDAY	TUESDAY	WEDNESDAY
	TODAY'S GOAL	TODAY'S GOAL	TODAY'S GOAL
	PRIORITIES	PRIORITIES	PRIORITIES
	1	1	1
	2	2	2
	3	3	3
	4am	4am	4am
	5am	5am	5am
	6am	6am	6am
	7am	7am	7am
	8am	8am	8am
	9am	9am	9am
	10am	10am	10am
	11am	11am	11am
	12am	12am	12am
	1pm	1pm	1pm
	2pm	2pm	2pm
	3pm	3pm	3pm
	4pm	4pm	4pm
	5pm	5pm	5pm
	6pm	6pm	6pm
	7pm	7pm	7pm
	9pm	9pm	9pm
	10pm	10pm	10pm

ERRANDS

POSITIVE PATTERNS

	S	M	T	W	T	F	S
PHYSICAL							
PERSONAL							
PROFESSIONAL							

EVOLVING
BEAUTY

THE PLANNER
ESSENTIAL TACTICS TO BEING
happy
&
SUCCESSFUL

THURSDAY		FRIDAY		SATURDAY		SUNDAY	
TODAY'S GOAL		TODAY'S GOAL		TODAY'S GOAL		TODAY'S GOAL	
PRIORITIES		PRIORITIES		PRIORITIES		PRIORITIES	
1		1		1		1	
2		2		2		2	
3		3		3		3	
4am		4am		4am		4am	
5am		5am		5am		5am	
6am		6am		6am		6am	
7am		7am		7am		7am	
8am		8am		8am		8am	
9am		9am		9am		9am	
10am		10am		10am		10am	
11am		11am		11am		11am	
12am		12am		12am		12am	
1pm		1pm		1pm		1pm	
2pm		2pm		2pm		2pm	
3pm		3pm		3pm		3pm	
4pm		4pm		4pm		4pm	
5pm		5pm		5pm		5pm	
6pm		6pm		6pm		6pm	
7pm		7pm		7pm		7pm	
9pm		9pm		9pm		9pm	
10pm		10pm		10pm		10pm	

DISTRACTIONS THIS WEEK	BIG IDEAS THIS WEEK

DATE:

THIS WEEK'S GOAL

THE PLANNER
ESSENTIAL TACTICS TO BEING
happy
& SUCCESSFUL

THIS WEEK'S PRIORITIES	MONDAY		TUESDAY		WEDNESDAY	
	TODAY'S GOAL		TODAY'S GOAL		TODAY'S GOAL	
	PRIORITIES		PRIORITIES		PRIORITIES	
	1		1		1	
	2		2		2	
	3		3		3	
	4am		4am		4am	
	5am		5am		5am	
	6am		6am		6am	
	7am		7am		7am	
	8am		8am		8am	
	9am		9am		9am	
	10am		10am		10am	
	11am		11am		11am	
	12am		12am		12am	
	1pm		1pm		1pm	
	2pm		2pm		2pm	
	3pm		3pm		3pm	
	4pm		4pm		4pm	
	5pm		5pm		5pm	
	6pm		6pm		6pm	
	7pm		7pm		7pm	
	9pm		9pm		9pm	
	10pm		10pm		10pm	

ERRANDS

POSITIVE PATTERNS		S	M	T	W	T	F	S
PHYSICAL								
PERSONAL								
PROFESSIONAL								

THURSDAY		FRIDAY		SATURDAY		SUNDAY	
TODAY'S GOAL		TODAY'S GOAL		TODAY'S GOAL		TODAY'S GOAL	
PRIORITIES		PRIORITIES		PRIORITIES		PRIORITIES	
1		1		1		1	
2		2		2		2	
3		3		3		3	
4am		4am		4am		4am	
5am		5am		5am		5am	
6am		6am		6am		6am	
7am		7am		7am		7am	
8am		8am		8am		8am	
9am		9am		9am		9am	
10am		10am		10am		10am	
11am		11am		11am		11am	
12am		12am		12am		12am	
1pm		1pm		1pm		1pm	
2pm		2pm		2pm		2pm	
3pm		3pm		3pm		3pm	
4pm		4pm		4pm		4pm	
5pm		5pm		5pm		5pm	
6pm		6pm		6pm		6pm	
7pm		7pm		7pm		7pm	
9pm		9pm		9pm		9pm	
10pm		10pm		10pm		10pm	

DISTRACTIONS THIS WEEK	BIG IDEAS THIS WEEK

MONTHLY REFLECTION

Visualize, in gratitude, Achieving Your Goals
Use the senses to see, hear, smell,
and touch the experience of what your success will look and feel like.

	MONTHLY GOAL	ACHIEVEMENT
1		
2		
3		

	PERSONAL	TIME SPENT	TACTICS FOR IMPROVEMENT
1			
2			
3			
	PROFESSIONAL		
1			
2			
3			
	PHYSICAL		
1			
2			
3			

1. WHAT DID I LEARN THIS MONTH?
1.
2.
3.
4.
5.

2. DISTRACTIONS AVOID / FEARS TO FORGE THROUGH
1.
2.
3.
4.
5.

3. PEOPLE I LEARNED FROM OR INSPIRED ME?
1.
2.
3.
4.
5.

4. MISSED OPPORTUNITIES THIS MONTH?
1.
2.
3.
4.
5.

5. WHAT ACTIONS CAN I CORRECT FOR NEXT MONTH?
1.
2.
3.
4.
5.

HOW DID I SPENT MY TIME THIS MONTH?
* KEEP BRAND MASTERY PRIORITIES &
PERSONAL STATEMENT TOP OF MIND.
WHAT YOU SAY AND DO SHOULD ALIGN.

PERSONAL
___% Time

PROFESSIONAL
___% Time

PHYSICAL
___% Time

NOTES

NOTES

ERICA DOUGLAS
BEAUTY PIONEER

" A WOMAN who does not require validation, is the most feared on the planet "

COSMETIC CHEMIST & CEO

ERICA DOUGLAS

Is a **BEAUTY PIONEER** on many levels. For starters, she's an African American woman, a cosmetic chemist and an ivy leaguer with a keen business acumen in the beauty industry. Erica understands that education is more than higher learning. "It provides access to resources and a network {a Tribe}. School teaches critical thinking and problem solving," Douglas explains. She develops products and provides services primarily to an underserved community of beauty entrepreneurs. Her intention is to increase woman and minority ownership in the beauty business landscape. This trailblazer is one to watch.

> " *Don't focus on making money, focus on creating value.* "

Sister Scientist

m.SEED *group*™

An experienced group of experts in the beauty space, providing services in contract manufacturing, research & product development, regulatory and marketing/branding strategy.

As a diverse team of specialists under one umbrella, we are aligned to eliminate constraints typically experienced by entrepreneurs, small businesses and growing brands.

My morning routine is... I wake up at 4:00 am and answer emails that I didn't get to the day before. This is the time I am most productive. I play gospel music from the time I wake up till I get into office.

How long have you been an entrepreneur?
I've been an entrepreneur for three years. I co-founded mSEED with two partners; Anthony Standifer and Barry Williams.

The hardest challenges the first year were?
Building a business while trying to find creative ways to earn personal income. Shifting my mindset to the "no hustle, no eat"concept. Finding "good help." Explaining to friends and family what I was doing and why.

How did you overcome the challenges....
By reducing living expenses and reducing frivolous spending (i.e. parties, travel, eating out, etc.) Networking and telling whoever would listen what we were doing. Word would spread and people started finding us. Doing what I said I would do so now people see the fruits of my labor and sacrifice.

One of the biggest mistakes young entrepreneurs / millennials make is... I believe they spend too much time talking about being an entrepreneur and teaching others how to, rather than investing more time in executing on their actual business.

How has the Digital Age changed your business? Highs/Lows?
It has allowed me to find, engage and communicate with my direct customer without {traditional} "advertising" to them. The problem with it is that everybody thinks they have access to me and my time.

I want my legacy to be...
That I am a game changer.

I AM AN OUTSPOKEN BUSINESS *SAVVY* GEEK

Erica Douglas is a Chicago, IL native. She holds a B.S. in Chemical Engineering from Stanford University and an MBA from Northwestern University. For more information go to www.SisterScientist.com | @SisterScientist | www.mSeedGroup.com

MY PERSONAL STATEMENT FOR THE YEAR

MONTH:

"The Beauty of the World lies in the Diversity of It's People. "--Unknown

SUNDAY	MONDAY	TUESDAY	WEDNESDAY	THURSDAY	FRIDAY	SATURDAY

GRATITUDES/NOTES

Visualize the completion of your Personal, Professional and Physical goals.
*Your monthly goals should align with your **Brand Mastery Priorities** from Step 1.*

My Personal Intention is...
1
2
3

My Professional Intention is...
1
2
3

My Physical Intention is...
1
2
3

DATE:

THIS WEEK'S GOAL

EVOLVING BEAUTY
THE PLANNER
ESSENTIAL TACTICS TO BEING
happy
& SUCCESSFUL

THIS WEEK'S PRIORITIES	MONDAY	TUESDAY	WEDNESDAY
	TODAY'S GOAL	TODAY'S GOAL	TODAY'S GOAL
	PRIORITIES	PRIORITIES	PRIORITIES
	1	1	1
	2	2	2
	3	3	3
	4am	4am	4am
	5am	5am	5am
	6am	6am	6am
	7am	7am	7am
	8am	8am	8am
	9am	9am	9am
	10am	10am	10am
	11am	11am	11am
	12am	12am	12am
	1pm	1pm	1pm
	2pm	2pm	2pm
	3pm	3pm	3pm
	4pm	4pm	4pm
	5pm	5pm	5pm
	6pm	6pm	6pm
	7pm	7pm	7pm
	9pm	9pm	9pm
	10pm	10pm	10pm

ERRANDS

POSITIVE PATTERNS

	S	M	T	W	T	F	S
PHYSICAL							
PERSONAL							
PROFESSIONAL							

THE PLANNER
ESSENTIAL TACTICS TO BEING
happy
& SUCCESSFUL

THURSDAY		FRIDAY		SATURDAY		SUNDAY	
TODAY'S GOAL		TODAY'S GOAL		TODAY'S GOAL		TODAY'S GOAL	
PRIORITIES		PRIORITIES		PRIORITIES		PRIORITIES	
1		1		1		1	
2		2		2		2	
3		3		3		3	
4am		4am		4am		4am	
5am		5am		5am		5am	
6am		6am		6am		6am	
7am		7am		7am		7am	
8am		8am		8am		8am	
9am		9am		9am		9am	
10am		10am		10am		10am	
11am		11am		11am		11am	
12am		12am		12am		12am	
1pm		1pm		1pm		1pm	
2pm		2pm		2pm		2pm	
3pm		3pm		3pm		3pm	
4pm		4pm		4pm		4pm	
5pm		5pm		5pm		5pm	
6pm		6pm		6pm		6pm	
7pm		7pm		7pm		7pm	
9pm		9pm		9pm		9pm	
10pm		10pm		10pm		10pm	

DISTRACTIONS THIS WEEK	BIG IDEAS THIS WEEK

DATE:

THIS WEEK'S GOAL

THIS WEEK'S PRIORITIES

MONDAY	TUESDAY	WEDNESDAY
TODAY'S GOAL	TODAY'S GOAL	TODAY'S GOAL
PRIORITIES	PRIORITIES	PRIORITIES
1	1	1
2	2	2
3	3	3
4am	4am	4am
5am	5am	5am
6am	6am	6am
7am	7am	7am
8am	8am	8am
9am	9am	9am
10am	10am	10am
11am	11am	11am
12am	12am	12am
1pm	1pm	1pm
2pm	2pm	2pm
3pm	3pm	3pm
4pm	4pm	4pm
5pm	5pm	5pm
6pm	6pm	6pm
7pm	7pm	7pm
9pm	9pm	9pm
10pm	10pm	10pm

ERRANDS

POSITIVE PATTERNS

	S	M	T	W	T	F	S
PHYSICAL							
PERSONAL							
PROFESSIONAL							

THE PLANNER
ESSENTIAL TACTICS TO BEING
happy
& SUCCESSFUL

THURSDAY		FRIDAY		SATURDAY		SUNDAY	
TODAY'S GOAL		TODAY'S GOAL		TODAY'S GOAL		TODAY'S GOAL	
PRIORITIES		PRIORITIES		PRIORITIES		PRIORITIES	
1		1		1		1	
2		2		2		2	
3		3		3		3	
4am		4am		4am		4am	
5am		5am		5am		5am	
6am		6am		6am		6am	
7am		7am		7am		7am	
8am		8am		8am		8am	
9am		9am		9am		9am	
10am		10am		10am		10am	
11am		11am		11am		11am	
12am		12am		12am		12am	
1pm		1pm		1pm		1pm	
2pm		2pm		2pm		2pm	
3pm		3pm		3pm		3pm	
4pm		4pm		4pm		4pm	
5pm		5pm		5pm		5pm	
6pm		6pm		6pm		6pm	
7pm		7pm		7pm		7pm	
9pm		9pm		9pm		9pm	
10pm		10pm		10pm		10pm	

DISTRACTIONS THIS WEEK	BIG IDEAS THIS WEEK

DATE:

THIS WEEK'S GOAL

EVOLVING BEAUTY

THE PLANNER
ESSENTIAL TACTICS TO BEING
happy
& SUCCESSFUL

THIS WEEK'S PRIORITIES	MONDAY	TUESDAY	WEDNESDAY
	TODAY'S GOAL	TODAY'S GOAL	TODAY'S GOAL
	PRIORITIES	PRIORITIES	PRIORITIES
	1	1	1
	2	2	2
	3	3	3
	4am	4am	4am
	5am	5am	5am
	6am	6am	6am
	7am	7am	7am
	8am	8am	8am
	9am	9am	9am
	10am	10am	10am
	11am	11am	11am
	12am	12am	12am
	1pm	1pm	1pm
	2pm	2pm	2pm
	3pm	3pm	3pm
	4pm	4pm	4pm
	5pm	5pm	5pm
	6pm	6pm	6pm
	7pm	7pm	7pm
	9pm	9pm	9pm
	10pm	10pm	10pm

ERRANDS

POSITIVE PATTERNS

	S	M	T	W	T	F	S
PHYSICAL							
PERSONAL							
PROFESSIONAL							

THE PLANNER

ESSENTIAL TACTICS TO BEING

happy
& SUCCESSFUL

THURSDAY		FRIDAY		SATURDAY		SUNDAY	
TODAY'S GOAL		TODAY'S GOAL		TODAY'S GOAL		TODAY'S GOAL	
PRIORITIES		PRIORITIES		PRIORITIES		PRIORITIES	
1		1		1		1	
2		2		2		2	
3		3		3		3	
4am		4am		4am		4am	
5am		5am		5am		5am	
6am		6am		6am		6am	
7am		7am		7am		7am	
8am		8am		8am		8am	
9am		9am		9am		9am	
10am		10am		10am		10am	
11am		11am		11am		11am	
12am		12am		12am		12am	
1pm		1pm		1pm		1pm	
2pm		2pm		2pm		2pm	
3pm		3pm		3pm		3pm	
4pm		4pm		4pm		4pm	
5pm		5pm		5pm		5pm	
6pm		6pm		6pm		6pm	
7pm		7pm		7pm		7pm	
9pm		9pm		9pm		9pm	
10pm		10pm		10pm		10pm	

DISTRACTIONS THIS WEEK	BIG IDEAS THIS WEEK

DATE:

EVOLVING
BEAUTY

THE PLANNER
ESSENTIAL TACTICS TO BEING
happy
& SUCCESSFUL

THIS WEEK'S PRIORITIES	MONDAY		TUESDAY		WEDNESDAY	
	TODAY'S GOAL		TODAY'S GOAL		TODAY'S GOAL	
	PRIORITIES		PRIORITIES		PRIORITIES	
	1		1		1	
	2		2		2	
	3		3		3	
	4am		4am		4am	
	5am		5am		5am	
	6am		6am		6am	
	7am		7am		7am	
	8am		8am		8am	
	9am		9am		9am	
	10am		10am		10am	
	11am		11am		11am	
	12am		12am		12am	
	1pm		1pm		1pm	
	2pm		2pm		2pm	
	3pm		3pm		3pm	
	4pm		4pm		4pm	
	5pm		5pm		5pm	
	6pm		6pm		6pm	
	7pm		7pm		7pm	
	9pm		9pm		9pm	
	10pm		10pm		10pm	

ERRANDS	POSITIVE PATTERNS						
		S	M	T	W	T	F	S
	PHYSICAL						
	PERSONAL						
	PROFESSIONAL						

THE PLANNER

ESSENTIAL TACTICS TO BEING

happy
& SUCCESSFUL

THURSDAY		FRIDAY		SATURDAY		SUNDAY	
TODAY'S GOAL		TODAY'S GOAL		TODAY'S GOAL		TODAY'S GOAL	
PRIORITIES		PRIORITIES		PRIORITIES		PRIORITIES	
1		1		1		1	
2		2		2		2	
3		3		3		3	
4am		4am		4am		4am	
5am		5am		5am		5am	
6am		6am		6am		6am	
7am		7am		7am		7am	
8am		8am		8am		8am	
9am		9am		9am		9am	
10am		10am		10am		10am	
11am		11am		11am		11am	
12am		12am		12am		12am	
1pm		1pm		1pm		1pm	
2pm		2pm		2pm		2pm	
3pm		3pm		3pm		3pm	
4pm		4pm		4pm		4pm	
5pm		5pm		5pm		5pm	
6pm		6pm		6pm		6pm	
7pm		7pm		7pm		7pm	
9pm		9pm		9pm		9pm	
10pm		10pm		10pm		10pm	

DISTRACTIONS THIS WEEK	BIG IDEAS THIS WEEK

DATE:

THIS WEEK'S GOAL

EVOLVING BEAUTY

THE PLANNER
ESSENTIAL TACTICS TO BEING
happy
& SUCCESSFUL

THIS WEEK'S PRIORITIES	MONDAY		TUESDAY		WEDNESDAY	
	TODAY'S GOAL		TODAY'S GOAL		TODAY'S GOAL	
	PRIORITIES		PRIORITIES		PRIORITIES	
	1		1		1	
	2		2		2	
	3		3		3	
	4am		4am		4am	
	5am		5am		5am	
	6am		6am		6am	
	7am		7am		7am	
	8am		8am		8am	
	9am		9am		9am	
	10am		10am		10am	
	11am		11am		11am	
	12am		12am		12am	
	1pm		1pm		1pm	
	2pm		2pm		2pm	
	3pm		3pm		3pm	
	4pm		4pm		4pm	
	5pm		5pm		5pm	
	6pm		6pm		6pm	
	7pm		7pm		7pm	
	9pm		9pm		9pm	
	10pm		10pm		10pm	

ERRANDS

POSITIVE PATTERNS

	S	M	T	W	T	F	S
PHYSICAL							
PERSONAL							
PROFESSIONAL							

THE PLANNER
ESSENTIAL TACTICS TO BEING
happy
& SUCCESSFUL

THURSDAY		FRIDAY		SATURDAY		SUNDAY	
TODAY'S GOAL		TODAY'S GOAL		TODAY'S GOAL		TODAY'S GOAL	
PRIORITIES		PRIORITIES		PRIORITIES		PRIORITIES	
1		1		1		1	
2		2		2		2	
3		3		3		3	
4am		4am		4am		4am	
5am		5am		5am		5am	
6am		6am		6am		6am	
7am		7am		7am		7am	
8am		8am		8am		8am	
9am		9am		9am		9am	
10am		10am		10am		10am	
11am		11am		11am		11am	
12am		12am		12am		12am	
1pm		1pm		1pm		1pm	
2pm		2pm		2pm		2pm	
3pm		3pm		3pm		3pm	
4pm		4pm		4pm		4pm	
5pm		5pm		5pm		5pm	
6pm		6pm		6pm		6pm	
7pm		7pm		7pm		7pm	
9pm		9pm		9pm		9pm	
10pm		10pm		10pm		10pm	

DISTRACTIONS THIS WEEK	BIG IDEAS THIS WEEK

MONTHLY REFLECTION

Visualize, in gratitude, Achieving Your Goals
Use the senses to see, hear, smell,
and touch the experience of what your success will look and feel like.

	MONTHLY GOAL	ACHIEVEMENT
1		
2		
3		

PERSONAL	TIME SPENT	TACTICS FOR IMPROVEMENT
1		
2		
3		
PROFESSIONAL		
1		
2		
3		
PHYSICAL		
1		
2		
3		

1. WHAT DID I LEARN THIS MONTH?
1.
2.
3.
4.
5.

2. DISTRACTIONS AVOID / FEARS TO FORGE THROUGH
1.
2.
3.
4.
5.

3. PEOPLE I LEARNED FROM OR INSPIRED ME?
1.
2.
3.
4.
5.

4. MISSED OPPORTUNITIES THIS MONTH?
1.
2.
3.
4.
5.

5. WHAT ACTIONS CAN I CORRECT FOR NEXT MONTH?
1.
2.
3.
4.
5.

HOW DID I SPENT MY TIME THIS MONTH?
* KEEP BRAND MASTERY PRIORITIES &
PERSONAL STATEMENT TOP OF MIND.
WHAT YOU SAY AND DO SHOULD ALIGN.

PERSONAL
___% Time

PROFESSIONAL
___% Time

PHYSICAL
___% Time

NOTES

NOTES

DANA HILL
THE NATURAL GIFTER

"Success is Not the Key to Happiness, Happiness is the Key to Success"

FOUNDER & CEO

DANA HILL

Is **THE NATURAL GIFTER**. She became an entrepreneur to create her own destiny; in 2004 she started Divine Marketing Group (DMG) a marketing and PR company. Cocotique launched in 2013, an evolution of DMG. Cocotique is fresh and considerate. It gives the gift of natural and organic beauty products.

My morning routine is...
I start my day with 10 minutes of meditation before checking emails. Although, this doesn't always happen..lol Then, I warm a small glass of Essentia alkaline water & add the lemon juice, Bragg's Apple Cider Vinegar, and a organic molasses. I drink this each morning before having my breakfast. It's detoxing, energizing and a great way to start the day!

I AM
LOVING
KIND
+
RESILIENT

My business is distinct because...
We focus on the importance of self-care and maintaining a healthy, balanced life. As women, we spend so much time caring for others, we tend to forget about ourselves. COCOTIQUE is self-care in a box and a great way for women to pamper themselves and have some "Me-Time." We also support women of color entrepreneurs by featuring their products in the box and providing a platform to increase their exposure and brand awareness in the marketplace.

I want my legacy to be...
Remembered as being loving, kind and compassionate to others, and that I inspired other women to realize their entrepreneurial or [career] dreams.

If I could tell my younger self something about being an entrepreneur...
Every little step you take towards building your business leads to realizing your goals. It's easy to become overwhelmed when you think of the end result. You have to take it one day at a time.

In the future, the beauty industry will...
Include more customized products: foundations to match diverse skin tones, and customized hair products to suit various hair textures. There are upcoming apps to match skin tones to existing lines.

⬤ COCOTIQUE

A deluxe beauty box subscription service for women of color. Each month 6-8 full or deluxe sample size beauty or lifestyle products are shipped to subscribers. Emerging, mass and prestige products. Beauty from every category– haircare, skincare, make-up, fragrance, nail polish and cosmetics. Everything Beauty!

Dana is a native of Pittsburg, PA. She graduated magna cum laude from American College in London, England, UK, with a BBA in Marketing. She currently resides in Cliffside Park, NJ. For more information go to Cocotique.com | @Cocotique.com.

MONTH:

MY PERSONAL STATEMENT FOR THE YEAR

EVOLVING BEAUTY

THE PLANNER
ESSENTIAL TACTICS TO BRING
happy
& SUCCESSFUL

"Surrender the Life You Have, Create the Life You Want." –PT

SUNDAY	MONDAY	TUESDAY	WEDNESDAY	THURSDAY	FRIDAY	SATURDAY

GRATITUDES/NOTES

Visualize the completion of your Personal, Professional and Physical goals.
*Your monthly goals should align with your **Brand Mastery Priorities** from Step 1.*

	My Personal Intention is…	
	1	
	2	
	3	
	My Professional Intention is…	
	1	
	2	
	3	
	My Physical Intention is…	
	1	
	2	
	3	

DATE:

EVOLVING BEAUTY

THE PLANNER
ESSENTIAL TACTICS TO BEING
happy
& SUCCESSFUL

THIS WEEK'S PRIORITIES	MONDAY	TUESDAY	WEDNESDAY
	TODAY'S GOAL	TODAY'S GOAL	TODAY'S GOAL
	PRIORITIES	PRIORITIES	PRIORITIES
	1	1	1
	2	2	2
	3	3	3
	4am	4am	4am
	5am	5am	5am
	6am	6am	6am
	7am	7am	7am
	8am	8am	8am
	9am	9am	9am
	10am	10am	10am
	11am	11am	11am
	12am	12am	12am
	1pm	1pm	1pm
	2pm	2pm	2pm
	3pm	3pm	3pm
	4pm	4pm	4pm
	5pm	5pm	5pm
	6pm	6pm	6pm
	7pm	7pm	7pm
	9pm	9pm	9pm
	10pm	10pm	10pm

ERRANDS

POSITIVE PATTERNS		S	M	T	W	T	F	S
PHYSICAL								
PERSONAL								
PROFESSIONAL								

THURSDAY		FRIDAY		SATURDAY		SUNDAY	
TODAY'S GOAL		TODAY'S GOAL		TODAY'S GOAL		TODAY'S GOAL	
PRIORITIES		PRIORITIES		PRIORITIES		PRIORITIES	
1		1		1		1	
2		2		2		2	
3		3		3		3	
4am		4am		4am		4am	
5am		5am		5am		5am	
6am		6am		6am		6am	
7am		7am		7am		7am	
8am		8am		8am		8am	
9am		9am		9am		9am	
10am		10am		10am		10am	
11am		11am		11am		11am	
12am		12am		12am		12am	
1pm		1pm		1pm		1pm	
2pm		2pm		2pm		2pm	
3pm		3pm		3pm		3pm	
4pm		4pm		4pm		4pm	
5pm		5pm		5pm		5pm	
6pm		6pm		6pm		6pm	
7pm		7pm		7pm		7pm	
9pm		9pm		9pm		9pm	
10pm		10pm		10pm		10pm	

DISTRACTIONS THIS WEEK	BIG IDEAS THIS WEEK

DATE:

THIS WEEK'S GOAL

THE PLANNER
ESSENTIAL TACTICS TO BEING
happy
& SUCCESSFUL

THIS WEEK'S PRIORITIES	MONDAY	TUESDAY	WEDNESDAY
	TODAY'S GOAL	TODAY'S GOAL	TODAY'S GOAL

	PRIORITIES		PRIORITIES		PRIORITIES	
	1		1		1	
	2		2		2	
	3		3		3	
	4am		4am		4am	
	5am		5am		5am	
	6am		6am		6am	
	7am		7am		7am	
	8am		8am		8am	
	9am		9am		9am	
	10am		10am		10am	
	11am		11am		11am	
	12am		12am		12am	
	1pm		1pm		1pm	
	2pm		2pm		2pm	
	3pm		3pm		3pm	
	4pm		4pm		4pm	
	5pm		5pm		5pm	
	6pm		6pm		6pm	
	7pm		7pm		7pm	
	9pm		9pm		9pm	
	10pm		10pm		10pm	

ERRANDS

POSITIVE PATTERNS							
	S	M	T	W	T	F	S
PHYSICAL							
PERSONAL							
PROFESSIONAL							

THE PLANNER
ESSENTIAL TACTICS TO BEING
happy
& SUCCESSFUL

THURSDAY		FRIDAY		SATURDAY		SUNDAY	
TODAY'S GOAL		TODAY'S GOAL		TODAY'S GOAL		TODAY'S GOAL	
PRIORITIES		PRIORITIES		PRIORITIES		PRIORITIES	
1		1		1		1	
2		2		2		2	
3		3		3		3	
4am		4am		4am		4am	
5am		5am		5am		5am	
6am		6am		6am		6am	
7am		7am		7am		7am	
8am		8am		8am		8am	
9am		9am		9am		9am	
10am		10am		10am		10am	
11am		11am		11am		11am	
12am		12am		12am		12am	
1pm		1pm		1pm		1pm	
2pm		2pm		2pm		2pm	
3pm		3pm		3pm		3pm	
4pm		4pm		4pm		4pm	
5pm		5pm		5pm		5pm	
6pm		6pm		6pm		6pm	
7pm		7pm		7pm		7pm	
9pm		9pm		9pm		9pm	
10pm		10pm		10pm		10pm	

DISTRACTIONS THIS WEEK	BIG IDEAS THIS WEEK

DATE:

THIS WEEK'S GOAL

THIS WEEK'S PRIORITIES	MONDAY	TUESDAY	WEDNESDAY
	TODAY'S GOAL	TODAY'S GOAL	TODAY'S GOAL

	PRIORITIES		PRIORITIES		PRIORITIES
	1		1		1
	2		2		2
	3		3		3
	4am		4am		4am
	5am		5am		5am
	6am		6am		6am
	7am		7am		7am
	8am		8am		8am
	9am		9am		9am
	10am		10am		10am
	11am		11am		11am
	12am		12am		12am
	1pm		1pm		1pm
	2pm		2pm		2pm
	3pm		3pm		3pm
	4pm		4pm		4pm
	5pm		5pm		5pm
	6pm		6pm		6pm
	7pm		7pm		7pm
	9pm		9pm		9pm
	10pm		10pm		10pm

ERRANDS

POSITIVE PATTERNS

	S	M	T	W	T	F	S
PHYSICAL							
PERSONAL							
PROFESSIONAL							

THE PLANNER
ESSENTIAL TACTICS TO BEING
happy
& SUCCESSFUL

THURSDAY		FRIDAY		SATURDAY		SUNDAY	
TODAY'S GOAL		TODAY'S GOAL		TODAY'S GOAL		TODAY'S GOAL	
PRIORITIES		PRIORITIES		PRIORITIES		PRIORITIES	
1		1		1		1	
2		2		2		2	
3		3		3		3	
4am		4am		4am		4am	
5am		5am		5am		5am	
6am		6am		6am		6am	
7am		7am		7am		7am	
8am		8am		8am		8am	
9am		9am		9am		9am	
10am		10am		10am		10am	
11am		11am		11am		11am	
12am		12am		12am		12am	
1pm		1pm		1pm		1pm	
2pm		2pm		2pm		2pm	
3pm		3pm		3pm		3pm	
4pm		4pm		4pm		4pm	
5pm		5pm		5pm		5pm	
6pm		6pm		6pm		6pm	
7pm		7pm		7pm		7pm	
9pm		9pm		9pm		9pm	
10pm		10pm		10pm		10pm	

DISTRACTIONS THIS WEEK	BIG IDEAS THIS WEEK

DATE:

THIS WEEK'S GOAL

THE PLANNER
ESSENTIAL TACTICS TO BEING
happy
& SUCCESSFUL

THIS WEEK'S PRIORITIES	MONDAY	TUESDAY	WEDNESDAY
	TODAY'S GOAL	TODAY'S GOAL	TODAY'S GOAL
	PRIORITIES	PRIORITIES	PRIORITIES
	1	1	1
	2	2	2
	3	3	3
	4am	4am	4am
	5am	5am	5am
	6am	6am	6am
	7am	7am	7am
	8am	8am	8am
	9am	9am	9am
	10am	10am	10am
	11am	11am	11am
	12am	12am	12am
	1pm	1pm	1pm
	2pm	2pm	2pm
	3pm	3pm	3pm
	4pm	4pm	4pm
	5pm	5pm	5pm
	6pm	6pm	6pm
	7pm	7pm	7pm
	9pm	9pm	9pm
	10pm	10pm	10pm

ERRANDS

POSITIVE PATTERNS

	S	M	T	W	T	F	S
PHYSICAL							
PERSONAL							
PROFESSIONAL							

THE PLANNER
ESSENTIAL TACTICS TO BEING
happy
&
SUCCESSFUL

THURSDAY		FRIDAY		SATURDAY		SUNDAY	
TODAY'S GOAL		TODAY'S GOAL		TODAY'S GOAL		TODAY'S GOAL	
PRIORITIES		PRIORITIES		PRIORITIES		PRIORITIES	
1		1		1		1	
2		2		2		2	
3		3		3		3	
4am		4am		4am		4am	
5am		5am		5am		5am	
6am		6am		6am		6am	
7am		7am		7am		7am	
8am		8am		8am		8am	
9am		9am		9am		9am	
10am		10am		10am		10am	
11am		11am		11am		11am	
12am		12am		12am		12am	
1pm		1pm		1pm		1pm	
2pm		2pm		2pm		2pm	
3pm		3pm		3pm		3pm	
4pm		4pm		4pm		4pm	
5pm		5pm		5pm		5pm	
6pm		6pm		6pm		6pm	
7pm		7pm		7pm		7pm	
9pm		9pm		9pm		9pm	
10pm		10pm		10pm		10pm	

DISTRACTIONS THIS WEEK	BIG IDEAS THIS WEEK

DATE:

EVOLVING
BEAUTY

THE PLANNER
ESSENTIAL TACTICS TO BEING
happy
& SUCCESSFUL

THIS WEEK'S PRIORITIES

MONDAY	TUESDAY	WEDNESDAY
TODAY'S GOAL	TODAY'S GOAL	TODAY'S GOAL

PRIORITIES	PRIORITIES	PRIORITIES
1	1	1
2	2	2
3	3	3
4am	4am	4am
5am	5am	5am
6am	6am	6am
7am	7am	7am
8am	8am	8am
9am	9am	9am
10am	10am	10am
11am	11am	11am
12am	12am	12am
1pm	1pm	1pm
2pm	2pm	2pm
3pm	3pm	3pm
4pm	4pm	4pm
5pm	5pm	5pm
6pm	6pm	6pm
7pm	7pm	7pm
9pm	9pm	9pm
10pm	10pm	10pm

ERRANDS

POSITIVE PATTERNS

	S	M	T	W	T	F	S
PHYSICAL							
PERSONAL							
PROFESSIONAL							

THURSDAY		FRIDAY		SATURDAY		SUNDAY	
TODAY'S GOAL		TODAY'S GOAL		TODAY'S GOAL		TODAY'S GOAL	
PRIORITIES		PRIORITIES		PRIORITIES		PRIORITIES	
1		1		1		1	
2		2		2		2	
3		3		3		3	
4am		4am		4am		4am	
5am		5am		5am		5am	
6am		6am		6am		6am	
7am		7am		7am		7am	
8am		8am		8am		8am	
9am		9am		9am		9am	
10am		10am		10am		10am	
11am		11am		11am		11am	
12am		12am		12am		12am	
1pm		1pm		1pm		1pm	
2pm		2pm		2pm		2pm	
3pm		3pm		3pm		3pm	
4pm		4pm		4pm		4pm	
5pm		5pm		5pm		5pm	
6pm		6pm		6pm		6pm	
7pm		7pm		7pm		7pm	
9pm		9pm		9pm		9pm	
10pm		10pm		10pm		10pm	

DISTRACTIONS THIS WEEK	BIG IDEAS THIS WEEK

MONTHLY REFLECTION

Visualize, in gratitude, Achieving Your Goals
*Use the senses to see, hear, smell,
and touch the experience of what your success will look and feel like.*

	MONTHLY GOAL		ACHIEVEMENT
1			
2			
3			

	PERSONAL	TIME SPENT	TACTICS FOR IMPROVEMENT
1			
2			
3			
	PROFESSIONAL		
1			
2			
3			
	PHYSICAL		
1			
2			
3			

1. WHAT DID I LEARN THIS MONTH?
1.
2.
3.
4.
5.

2. DISTRACTIONS AVOID / FEARS TO FORGE THROUGH
1.
2.
3.
4.
5.

3. PEOPLE I LEARNED FROM OR INSPIRED ME?
1.
2.
3.
4.
5.

4. MISSED OPPORTUNITIES THIS MONTH?
1.
2.
3.
4.
5.

5. WHAT ACTIONS CAN I CORRECT FOR NEXT MONTH?
1.
2.
3.
4.
5.

HOW DID I SPENT MY TIME THIS MONTH?
* KEEP BRAND MASTERY PRIORITIES &
PERSONAL STATEMENT TOP OF MIND.
WHAT YOU SAY AND DO SHOULD ALIGN.

PERSONAL
___% Time

PROFESSIONAL
___% Time

PHYSICAL
___% Time

NOTES

NOTES

SOPHIA WHITE
THE NAIL ARTIST

*"Have the Courage
to
Have Courage"*

CEO & MEDIA CORRESPONDENT

sophia!

SOPHIA WHITE

Is a **LICENSED NAIL TECH, ARTIST, RENAISSANCE WOMAN and a REAL BEAUTY** inside and out. She's also an Entrepreneur, Author, Media Correspondent and Model Spokesperson. Artists like Sophia need tribal support as they creatively navigate the world. And this beauty has a tribe of love. White, a self-proclaimed serial entrepreneur affirms, "I'm grateful for the [tribe of] family and friends I have that support and believe in all of my endeavors. In that respect I'm extremely blessed.

My morning routine is... Up at 5:00 am. Insanity Workout, a quick carrot, kale and apple juice or hot tea. I then get myself together, wake up my son, get him off to school and start my day at 8:30 am.

I started my own business because... I couldn't see myself working for someone my whole life or depending on someone else.

On Work/Life Balance... Be happy in working towards the things you love, but never sacrifice those you love.

I love the beauty industry because... It's the one industry that "specializes in the art" of being a Woman. It's constantly evolving with new ways to look and feel more amazing than the day before.

How has the Digital Age changed your business? The Digital Age has added "appeal" to the nail industry. You can see the latest trends around the world that you didn't know existed. You can communicate and learn from online video tutorials and other artists. The downside is techniques are constantly changing, often making it challenging to keep up. Master one trend before moving to the next. Sometimes it can be difficult, but you figure it out and give the client what they are looking for.

sophia!

"Push Through It. It Gets Better."

Splatter Mobile Nails is a division of Sophia White Brands. A mobile manicure service, which specializes in contemporary, fashion-forward nail art. We eliminate the commute time and provide the same services rendered in a nail salon, in the comfort of a home or office environment.

I AM
UNAPOLOGETIC
UNAPOLOGETIC
+ CONSISTENT

Sophia is originally from Buffalo, NY,. She's lived in France, Sweden and Greece. Today Sophia resides in New York City.
For more info go to
IAMSOPHIAWHITE.COM
@SophiainHarlem.

MONTH:

MY PERSONAL STATEMENT FOR THE YEAR

THE PLANNER
ESSENTIAL TACTICS TO BEING
happy
& SUCCESSFUL

"*You have within you the strength, the patience and the passion to reach for the stars to change the world.*" - H. Tubman

SUNDAY	MONDAY	TUESDAY	WEDNESDAY	THURSDAY	FRIDAY	SATURDAY

GRATITUDES/NOTES

Visualize the completion of your Personal, Professional and Physical goals.
*Your monthly goals should align with your **Brand Mastery Priorities** from Step 1.*

	My Personal Intention is...	1
		2
		3
	My Professional Intention is...	1
		2
		3
	My Physical Intention is....	1
		2
		3

DATE:

EVOLVING BEAUTY

THE PLANNER
ESSENTIAL TACTICS TO BEING
happy
& SUCCESSFUL

THIS WEEK'S PRIORITIES	MONDAY	TUESDAY	WEDNESDAY
	TODAY'S GOAL	TODAY'S GOAL	TODAY'S GOAL
	PRIORITIES	PRIORITIES	PRIORITIES
	1	1	1
	2	2	2
	3	3	3
	4am	4am	4am
	5am	5am	5am
	6am	6am	6am
	7am	7am	7am
	8am	8am	8am
	9am	9am	9am
	10am	10am	10am
	11am	11am	11am
	12am	12am	12am
	1pm	1pm	1pm
	2pm	2pm	2pm
	3pm	3pm	3pm
	4pm	4pm	4pm
	5pm	5pm	5pm
	6pm	6pm	6pm
	7pm	7pm	7pm
	9pm	9pm	9pm
	10pm	10pm	10pm

ERRANDS

POSITIVE PATTERNS	S	M	T	W	T	F	S
PHYSICAL							
PERSONAL							
PROFESSIONAL							

THE PLANNER

ESSENTIAL TACTICS TO BEING

happy & SUCCESSFUL

THURSDAY		FRIDAY		SATURDAY		SUNDAY	
TODAY'S GOAL		TODAY'S GOAL		TODAY'S GOAL		TODAY'S GOAL	
PRIORITIES		PRIORITIES		PRIORITIES		PRIORITIES	
1		1		1		1	
2		2		2		2	
3		3		3		3	
4am		4am		4am		4am	
5am		5am		5am		5am	
6am		6am		6am		6am	
7am		7am		7am		7am	
8am		8am		8am		8am	
9am		9am		9am		9am	
10am		10am		10am		10am	
11am		11am		11am		11am	
12am		12am		12am		12am	
1pm		1pm		1pm		1pm	
2pm		2pm		2pm		2pm	
3pm		3pm		3pm		3pm	
4pm		4pm		4pm		4pm	
5pm		5pm		5pm		5pm	
6pm		6pm		6pm		6pm	
7pm		7pm		7pm		7pm	
9pm		9pm		9pm		9pm	
10pm		10pm		10pm		10pm	

DISTRACTIONS THIS WEEK	BIG IDEAS THIS WEEK

151

DATE:

THIS WEEK'S GOAL

THIS WEEK'S PRIORITIES	MONDAY	TUESDAY	WEDNESDAY
	TODAY'S GOAL	TODAY'S GOAL	TODAY'S GOAL
	PRIORITIES	PRIORITIES	PRIORITIES
	1	1	1
	2	2	2
	3	3	3
	4am	4am	4am
	5am	5am	5am
	6am	6am	6am
	7am	7am	7am
	8am	8am	8am
	9am	9am	9am
	10am	10am	10am
	11am	11am	11am
	12am	12am	12am
	1pm	1pm	1pm
	2pm	2pm	2pm
	3pm	3pm	3pm
	4pm	4pm	4pm
	5pm	5pm	5pm
	6pm	6pm	6pm
	7pm	7pm	7pm
	9pm	9pm	9pm
	10pm	10pm	10pm

ERRANDS

POSITIVE PATTERNS

	S	M	T	W	T	F	S
PHYSICAL							
PERSONAL							
PROFESSIONAL							

THURSDAY		FRIDAY		SATURDAY		SUNDAY	
TODAY'S GOAL		TODAY'S GOAL		TODAY'S GOAL		TODAY'S GOAL	
PRIORITIES		PRIORITIES		PRIORITIES		PRIORITIES	
1		1		1		1	
2		2		2		2	
3		3		3		3	
4am		4am		4am		4am	
5am		5am		5am		5am	
6am		6am		6am		6am	
7am		7am		7am		7am	
8am		8am		8am		8am	
9am		9am		9am		9am	
10am		10am		10am		10am	
11am		11am		11am		11am	
12am		12am		12am		12am	
1pm		1pm		1pm		1pm	
2pm		2pm		2pm		2pm	
3pm		3pm		3pm		3pm	
4pm		4pm		4pm		4pm	
5pm		5pm		5pm		5pm	
6pm		6pm		6pm		6pm	
7pm		7pm		7pm		7pm	
9pm		9pm		9pm		9pm	
10pm		10pm		10pm		10pm	

DISTRACTIONS THIS WEEK	BIG IDEAS THIS WEEK

153

DATE:

THIS WEEK'S GOAL

EVOLVING
BEAUTY

THE PLANNER
ESSENTIAL TACTICS TO BEING
happy
& SUCCESSFUL

THIS WEEK'S PRIORITIES	

MONDAY	TUESDAY	WEDNESDAY
TODAY'S GOAL	TODAY'S GOAL	TODAY'S GOAL
PRIORITIES	PRIORITIES	PRIORITIES
1	1	1
2	2	2
3	3	3
4am	4am	4am
5am	5am	5am
6am	6am	6am
7am	7am	7am
8am	8am	8am
9am	9am	9am
10am	10am	10am
11am	11am	11am
12am	12am	12am
1pm	1pm	1pm
2pm	2pm	2pm
3pm	3pm	3pm
4pm	4pm	4pm
5pm	5pm	5pm
6pm	6pm	6pm
7pm	7pm	7pm
9pm	9pm	9pm
10pm	10pm	10pm

ERRANDS

POSITIVE PATTERNS

	S	M	T	W	T	F	S
PHYSICAL							
PERSONAL							
PROFESSIONAL							

THE PLANNER

ESSENTIAL TACTICS TO BEING

happy
& SUCCESSFUL

THURSDAY		FRIDAY		SATURDAY		SUNDAY	
TODAY'S GOAL		TODAY'S GOAL		TODAY'S GOAL		TODAY'S GOAL	
PRIORITIES		PRIORITIES		PRIORITIES		PRIORITIES	
1		1		1		1	
2		2		2		2	
3		3		3		3	
4am		4am		4am		4am	
5am		5am		5am		5am	
6am		6am		6am		6am	
7am		7am		7am		7am	
8am		8am		8am		8am	
9am		9am		9am		9am	
10am		10am		10am		10am	
11am		11am		11am		11am	
12am		12am		12am		12am	
1pm		1pm		1pm		1pm	
2pm		2pm		2pm		2pm	
3pm		3pm		3pm		3pm	
4pm		4pm		4pm		4pm	
5pm		5pm		5pm		5pm	
6pm		6pm		6pm		6pm	
7pm		7pm		7pm		7pm	
9pm		9pm		9pm		9pm	
10pm		10pm		10pm		10pm	

DISTRACTIONS THIS WEEK	BIG IDEAS THIS WEEK

DATE:

THIS WEEK'S GOAL

THIS WEEK'S PRIORITIES	MONDAY		TUESDAY		WEDNESDAY	
	TODAY'S GOAL		TODAY'S GOAL		TODAY'S GOAL	
	PRIORITIES		PRIORITIES		PRIORITIES	
	1		1		1	
	2		2		2	
	3		3		3	
	4am		4am		4am	
	5am		5am		5am	
	6am		6am		6am	
	7am		7am		7am	
	8am		8am		8am	
	9am		9am		9am	
	10am		10am		10am	
	11am		11am		11am	
	12am		12am		12am	
	1pm		1pm		1pm	
	2pm		2pm		2pm	
	3pm		3pm		3pm	
	4pm		4pm		4pm	
	5pm		5pm		5pm	
	6pm		6pm		6pm	
	7pm		7pm		7pm	
	9pm		9pm		9pm	
	10pm		10pm		10pm	

ERRANDS

POSITIVE PATTERNS	S	M	T	W	T	F	S
PHYSICAL							
PERSONAL							
PROFESSIONAL							

156

THURSDAY		FRIDAY		SATURDAY		SUNDAY	
TODAY'S GOAL		TODAY'S GOAL		TODAY'S GOAL		TODAY'S GOAL	
PRIORITIES		**PRIORITIES**		**PRIORITIES**		**PRIORITIES**	
1		1		1		1	
2		2		2		2	
3		3		3		3	
4am		4am		4am		4am	
5am		5am		5am		5am	
6am		6am		6am		6am	
7am		7am		7am		7am	
8am		8am		8am		8am	
9am		9am		9am		9am	
10am		10am		10am		10am	
11am		11am		11am		11am	
12am		12am		12am		12am	
1pm		1pm		1pm		1pm	
2pm		2pm		2pm		2pm	
3pm		3pm		3pm		3pm	
4pm		4pm		4pm		4pm	
5pm		5pm		5pm		5pm	
6pm		6pm		6pm		6pm	
7pm		7pm		7pm		7pm	
9pm		9pm		9pm		9pm	
10pm		10pm		10pm		10pm	

DISTRACTIONS THIS WEEK	BIG IDEAS THIS WEEK

DATE:

THIS WEEK'S GOAL

EVOLVING
BEAUTY

THE PLANNER
ESSENTIAL TACTICS TO BEING
happy
& SUCCESSFUL

THIS WEEK'S PRIORITIES	MONDAY	TUESDAY	WEDNESDAY
	TODAY'S GOAL	TODAY'S GOAL	TODAY'S GOAL

	PRIORITIES	PRIORITIES	PRIORITIES
	1	1	1
	2	2	2
	3	3	3
	4am	4am	4am
	5am	5am	5am
	6am	6am	6am
	7am	7am	7am
	8am	8am	8am
	9am	9am	9am
	10am	10am	10am
	11am	11am	11am
	12am	12am	12am
	1pm	1pm	1pm
	2pm	2pm	2pm
	3pm	3pm	3pm
	4pm	4pm	4pm
	5pm	5pm	5pm
	6pm	6pm	6pm
	7pm	7pm	7pm
	9pm	9pm	9pm
	10pm	10pm	10pm

ERRANDS

POSITIVE PATTERNS

	S	M	T	W	T	F	S
PHYSICAL							
PERSONAL							
PROFESSIONAL							

THE PLANNER
ESSENTIAL TACTICS TO BEING
happy
& SUCCESSFUL

THURSDAY		FRIDAY		SATURDAY		SUNDAY	
TODAY'S GOAL		TODAY'S GOAL		TODAY'S GOAL		TODAY'S GOAL	
PRIORITIES		PRIORITIES		PRIORITIES		PRIORITIES	
1		1		1		1	
2		2		2		2	
3		3		3		3	
4am		4am		4am		4am	
5am		5am		5am		5am	
6am		6am		6am		6am	
7am		7am		7am		7am	
8am		8am		8am		8am	
9am		9am		9am		9am	
10am		10am		10am		10am	
11am		11am		11am		11am	
12am		12am		12am		12am	
1pm		1pm		1pm		1pm	
2pm		2pm		2pm		2pm	
3pm		3pm		3pm		3pm	
4pm		4pm		4pm		4pm	
5pm		5pm		5pm		5pm	
6pm		6pm		6pm		6pm	
7pm		7pm		7pm		7pm	
9pm		9pm		9pm		9pm	
10pm		10pm		10pm		10pm	

DISTRACTIONS THIS WEEK	BIG IDEAS THIS WEEK

159

MONTHLY REFLECTION

Visualize, in gratitude, Achieving Your Goals
*Use the senses to see, hear, smell,
and touch the experience of what your success will look and feel like.*

	MONTHLY GOAL		ACHIEVEMENT
1			
2			
3			

	PERSONAL	TIME SPENT	TACTICS FOR IMPROVEMENT
1			
2			
3			
	PROFESSIONAL		
1			
2			
3			
	PHYSICAL		
1			
2			
3			

1. WHAT DID I LEARN THIS MONTH?
1.
2.
3.
4.
5.

2. DISTRACTIONS AVOID / FEARS TO FORGE THROUGH
1.
2.
3.
4.
5.

3. PEOPLE I LEARNED FROM OR INSPIRED ME?
1.
2.
3.
4.
5.

4. MISSED OPPORTUNITIES THIS MONTH?
1.
2.
3.
4.
5.

5. WHAT ACTIONS CAN I CORRECT FOR NEXT MONTH?
1.
2.
3.
4.
5.

HOW DID I SPENT MY TIME THIS MONTH?
* KEEP BRAND MASTERY PRIORITIES &
PERSONAL STATEMENT TOP OF MIND.
WHAT YOU SAY AND DO SHOULD ALIGN.

PERSONAL
___% Time

PROFESSIONAL
___% Time

PHYSICAL
___% Time

NOTES

NOTES

162

JAE NASH
THE VOICE OF INSPIRATION

*"Keep Your Head
In the Game &
Surround Yourself
with Positive
People"*

CEO & MEDIA CORRESPONDENT

JAE NASH

Is THE VOICE OF INSPIRATION. "I couldn't see myself working for anyone else." Nash explains. A woman-centric, serial entrepreneur of 10 years. Her business and life experiences serve as a muse for women, wives, mothers and female entrepreneurs. Today, the resilient Nash is the Host & CEO of a radio show she created, Girl Power Hour, Inspiration for Women Living on Purpose.

I AM
BEAUTIFUL
BOLD
+ COURAGEOUS

An international-reaching syndicated radio show that entertains, enlightens, encourages, & equips women to live and thrive in their uniquely-designed purpose & identity.

We're a community of women who are driven to living a lifestyle of purpose, on purpose, by way of evolving into a better version of ourselves daily!

My morning routine is... Getting my daughter up for school, helping her with her hygiene routine, praying together, then getting myself off to work. In that order.

I love the beauty industry because... It allows you to transform into many different alter egos.

How has the Digital Age changed your business? Highs/Low: It has given talented people so much exposure & an incredible ease in obtaining it; however, these newly "famous" personalities have overwhelmed the digital space with almost too much exposure to the point that it's unnecessarily overcrowded.

The best advice I ever received is... Change the way you think--it'll change your life. **On work/life balance...** Learn to unplug when needed. Take care of yourself: Mind, Body, & Spirit.

One of the biggest mistakes millennials make... I believe some think there is a shortcut to success. There is no easy route. Put in the hard work and reap the rewards.

I want my legacy to be... How much I gave back, financially & otherwise, to causes that are changing lives, like TheCauseCulture.org.

Jae Nash is a native of Indianapolis, Indiana. She has a certification in Radio & Television Broadcasting from the Atlanta Broadcast Institute. She resides in a suburb of Atlanta, Ga. For more information go to GirlPowerHourRadio.com, LIVE on Fridays at 11 am. EST | @GirlPowerHour | @GirlPower_Hour

EVOLVING BEAUTY

THE PLANNER
ESSENTIAL TACTICS TO BEING
happy
& SUCCESSFUL

MY PERSONAL STATEMENT FOR THE YEAR

MONTH:

"Individually We Are One Drop, Together We're An Ocean" --Chole and Halle

SUNDAY	MONDAY	TUESDAY	WEDNESDAY	THURSDAY	FRIDAY	SATURDAY

Visualize the completion of your Personal, Professional and Physical goals.
*Your monthly goals should align with your **Brand Mastery Priorities** from Step 1.*

My Personal Intention is...
1
2
3

My Professional Intention is...
1
2
3

My Physical Intention is...
1
2
3

GRATITUDES/NOTES

DATE:

THIS WEEK'S GOAL

THIS WEEK'S PRIORITIES	MONDAY	TUESDAY	WEDNESDAY
	TODAY'S GOAL	TODAY'S GOAL	TODAY'S GOAL
	PRIORITIES	PRIORITIES	PRIORITIES
	1	1	1
	2	2	2
	3	3	3
	4am	4am	4am
	5am	5am	5am
	6am	6am	6am
	7am	7am	7am
	8am	8am	8am
	9am	9am	9am
	10am	10am	10am
	11am	11am	11am
	12am	12am	12am
	1pm	1pm	1pm
	2pm	2pm	2pm
	3pm	3pm	3pm
	4pm	4pm	4pm
	5pm	5pm	5pm
	6pm	6pm	6pm
	7pm	7pm	7pm
	9pm	9pm	9pm
	10pm	10pm	10pm

ERRANDS	POSITIVE PATTERNS							
		S	M	T	W	T	F	S
	PHYSICAL							
	PERSONAL							
	PROFESSIONAL							

THURSDAY		FRIDAY		SATURDAY		SUNDAY	
TODAY'S GOAL		TODAY'S GOAL		TODAY'S GOAL		TODAY'S GOAL	
PRIORITIES		PRIORITIES		PRIORITIES		PRIORITIES	
1		1		1		1	
2		2		2		2	
3		3		3		3	
4am		4am		4am		4am	
5am		5am		5am		5am	
6am		6am		6am		6am	
7am		7am		7am		7am	
8am		8am		8am		8am	
9am		9am		9am		9am	
10am		10am		10am		10am	
11am		11am		11am		11am	
12am		12am		12am		12am	
1pm		1pm		1pm		1pm	
2pm		2pm		2pm		2pm	
3pm		3pm		3pm		3pm	
4pm		4pm		4pm		4pm	
5pm		5pm		5pm		5pm	
6pm		6pm		6pm		6pm	
7pm		7pm		7pm		7pm	
9pm		9pm		9pm		9pm	
10pm		10pm		10pm		10pm	

DISTRACTIONS THIS WEEK	BIG IDEAS THIS WEEK

DATE:

THIS WEEK'S GOAL

THE PLANNER
ESSENTIAL TACTICS TO BEING
happy
& SUCCESSFUL

THIS WEEK'S PRIORITIES

MONDAY	TUESDAY	WEDNESDAY
TODAY'S GOAL	TODAY'S GOAL	TODAY'S GOAL

PRIORITIES	PRIORITIES	PRIORITIES
1	1	1
2	2	2
3	3	3
4am	4am	4am
5am	5am	5am
6am	6am	6am
7am	7am	7am
8am	8am	8am
9am	9am	9am
10am	10am	10am
11am	11am	11am
12am	12am	12am
1pm	1pm	1pm
2pm	2pm	2pm
3pm	3pm	3pm
4pm	4pm	4pm
5pm	5pm	5pm
6pm	6pm	6pm
7pm	7pm	7pm
9pm	9pm	9pm
10pm	10pm	10pm

ERRANDS

POSITIVE PATTERNS

	S	M	T	W	T	F	S
PHYSICAL							
PERSONAL							
PROFESSIONAL							

THE PLANNER
ESSENTIAL TACTICS TO BEING
happy
& SUCCESSFUL

THURSDAY		FRIDAY		SATURDAY		SUNDAY	
TODAY'S GOAL		TODAY'S GOAL		TODAY'S GOAL		TODAY'S GOAL	
PRIORITIES		PRIORITIES		PRIORITIES		PRIORITIES	
1		1		1		1	
2		2		2		2	
3		3		3		3	
4am		4am		4am		4am	
5am		5am		5am		5am	
6am		6am		6am		6am	
7am		7am		7am		7am	
8am		8am		8am		8am	
9am		9am		9am		9am	
10am		10am		10am		10am	
11am		11am		11am		11am	
12am		12am		12am		12am	
1pm		1pm		1pm		1pm	
2pm		2pm		2pm		2pm	
3pm		3pm		3pm		3pm	
4pm		4pm		4pm		4pm	
5pm		5pm		5pm		5pm	
6pm		6pm		6pm		6pm	
7pm		7pm		7pm		7pm	
9pm		9pm		9pm		9pm	
10pm		10pm		10pm		10pm	

DISTRACTIONS THIS WEEK	BIG IDEAS THIS WEEK

DATE:

THIS WEEK'S GOAL

EVOLVING BEAUTY

THE PLANNER
ESSENTIAL TACTICS TO BEING
happy
& SUCCESSFUL

THIS WEEK'S PRIORITIES	MONDAY		TUESDAY		WEDNESDAY	
	TODAY'S GOAL		TODAY'S GOAL		TODAY'S GOAL	
	PRIORITIES		PRIORITIES		PRIORITIES	
	1		1		1	
	2		2		2	
	3		3		3	
	4am		4am		4am	
	5am		5am		5am	
	6am		6am		6am	
	7am		7am		7am	
	8am		8am		8am	
	9am		9am		9am	
	10am		10am		10am	
	11am		11am		11am	
	12am		12am		12am	
	1pm		1pm		1pm	
	2pm		2pm		2pm	
	3pm		3pm		3pm	
	4pm		4pm		4pm	
	5pm		5pm		5pm	
	6pm		6pm		6pm	
	7pm		7pm		7pm	
	9pm		9pm		9pm	
	10pm		10pm		10pm	

ERRANDS

POSITIVE PATTERNS

	S	M	T	W	T	F	S
PHYSICAL							
PERSONAL							
PROFESSIONAL							

THURSDAY		FRIDAY		SATURDAY		SUNDAY	
TODAY'S GOAL		TODAY'S GOAL		TODAY'S GOAL		TODAY'S GOAL	
PRIORITIES		PRIORITIES		PRIORITIES		PRIORITIES	
1		1		1		1	
2		2		2		2	
3		3		3		3	
4am		4am		4am		4am	
5am		5am		5am		5am	
6am		6am		6am		6am	
7am		7am		7am		7am	
8am		8am		8am		8am	
9am		9am		9am		9am	
10am		10am		10am		10am	
11am		11am		11am		11am	
12am		12am		12am		12am	
1pm		1pm		1pm		1pm	
2pm		2pm		2pm		2pm	
3pm		3pm		3pm		3pm	
4pm		4pm		4pm		4pm	
5pm		5pm		5pm		5pm	
6pm		6pm		6pm		6pm	
7pm		7pm		7pm		7pm	
9pm		9pm		9pm		9pm	
10pm		10pm		10pm		10pm	

DISTRACTIONS THIS WEEK	BIG IDEAS THIS WEEK

171

DATE:

THIS WEEK'S GOAL

THIS WEEK'S PRIORITIES		MONDAY		TUESDAY		WEDNESDAY	
		TODAY'S GOAL		TODAY'S GOAL		TODAY'S GOAL	
		PRIORITIES		PRIORITIES		PRIORITIES	
		1		1		1	
		2		2		2	
		3		3		3	
		4am		4am		4am	
		5am		5am		5am	
		6am		6am		6am	
		7am		7am		7am	
		8am		8am		8am	
		9am		9am		9am	
		10am		10am		10am	
		11am		11am		11am	
		12am		12am		12am	
		1pm		1pm		1pm	
		2pm		2pm		2pm	
		3pm		3pm		3pm	
		4pm		4pm		4pm	
		5pm		5pm		5pm	
		6pm		6pm		6pm	
		7pm		7pm		7pm	
		9pm		9pm		9pm	
		10pm		10pm		10pm	

ERRANDS	POSITIVE PATTERNS						
		S	M	T	W	T	F	S
	PHYSICAL							
	PERSONAL							
	PROFESSIONAL							

THE PLANNER
ESSENTIAL TACTICS TO BEING
happy
& SUCCESSFUL

THURSDAY		FRIDAY		SATURDAY		SUNDAY	
TODAY'S GOAL		TODAY'S GOAL		TODAY'S GOAL		TODAY'S GOAL	
PRIORITIES		**PRIORITIES**		**PRIORITIES**		**PRIORITIES**	
1		1		1		1	
2		2		2		2	
3		3		3		3	
4am		4am		4am		4am	
5am		5am		5am		5am	
6am		6am		6am		6am	
7am		7am		7am		7am	
8am		8am		8am		8am	
9am		9am		9am		9am	
10am		10am		10am		10am	
11am		11am		11am		11am	
12am		12am		12am		12am	
1pm		1pm		1pm		1pm	
2pm		2pm		2pm		2pm	
3pm		3pm		3pm		3pm	
4pm		4pm		4pm		4pm	
5pm		5pm		5pm		5pm	
6pm		6pm		6pm		6pm	
7pm		7pm		7pm		7pm	
9pm		9pm		9pm		9pm	
10pm		10pm		10pm		10pm	

DISTRACTIONS THIS WEEK	BIG IDEAS THIS WEEK

DATE:

THIS WEEK'S GOAL

THE PLANNER
ESSENTIAL TACTICS TO BEING
happy
& SUCCESSFUL

THIS WEEK'S PRIORITIES	MONDAY	TUESDAY	WEDNESDAY
	TODAY'S GOAL	TODAY'S GOAL	TODAY'S GOAL
	PRIORITIES	PRIORITIES	PRIORITIES
	1	1	1
	2	2	2
	3	3	3
	4am	4am	4am
	5am	5am	5am
	6am	6am	6am
	7am	7am	7am
	8am	8am	8am
	9am	9am	9am
	10am	10am	10am
	11am	11am	11am
	12am	12am	12am
	1pm	1pm	1pm
	2pm	2pm	2pm
	3pm	3pm	3pm
	4pm	4pm	4pm
	5pm	5pm	5pm
	6pm	6pm	6pm
	7pm	7pm	7pm
	9pm	9pm	9pm
	10pm	10pm	10pm

ERRANDS

POSITIVE PATTERNS

	S	M	T	W	T	F	S
PHYSICAL							
PERSONAL							
PROFESSIONAL							

THE PLANNER
ESSENTIAL TACTICS TO BEING
happy
& SUCCESSFUL

THURSDAY		FRIDAY		SATURDAY		SUNDAY	
TODAY'S GOAL		TODAY'S GOAL		TODAY'S GOAL		TODAY'S GOAL	
PRIORITIES		PRIORITIES		PRIORITIES		PRIORITIES	
1		1		1		1	
2		2		2		2	
3		3		3		3	
4am		4am		4am		4am	
5am		5am		5am		5am	
6am		6am		6am		6am	
7am		7am		7am		7am	
8am		8am		8am		8am	
9am		9am		9am		9am	
10am		10am		10am		10am	
11am		11am		11am		11am	
12am		12am		12am		12am	
1pm		1pm		1pm		1pm	
2pm		2pm		2pm		2pm	
3pm		3pm		3pm		3pm	
4pm		4pm		4pm		4pm	
5pm		5pm		5pm		5pm	
6pm		6pm		6pm		6pm	
7pm		7pm		7pm		7pm	
9pm		9pm		9pm		9pm	
10pm		10pm		10pm		10pm	

DISTRACTIONS THIS WEEK	BIG IDEAS THIS WEEK

MONTHLY REFLECTION

Visualize, in gratitude, Achieving Your Goals
*Use the senses to see, hear, smell,
and touch the experience of what your success will look and feel like.*

	MONTHLY GOAL		ACHIEVEMENT
1			
2			
3			

	PERSONAL	TIME SPENT	TACTICS FOR IMPROVEMENT
1			
2			
3			
	PROFESSIONAL		
1			
2			
3			
	PHYSICAL		
1			
2			
3			

1. WHAT DID I LEARN THIS MONTH?
1.
2.
3.
4.
5.

2. DISTRACTIONS AVOID / FEARS TO FORGE THROUGH
1.
2.
3.
4.
5.

3. PEOPLE I LEARNED FROM OR INSPIRED ME?
1.
2.
3.
4.
5.

4. MISSED OPPORTUNITIES THIS MONTH?
1.
2.
3.
4.
5.

5. WHAT ACTIONS CAN I CORRECT FOR NEXT MONTH?
1.
2.
3.
4.
5.

HOW DID I SPENT MY TIME THIS MONTH?
* KEEP BRAND MASTERY PRIORITIES &
PERSONAL STATEMENT TOP OF MIND.
WHAT YOU SAY AND DO SHOULD ALIGN.

PERSONAL
___% Time

PROFESSIONAL
___% Time

PHYSICAL
___% Time

NOTES

NOTES

TANYA GALLAGHER
THE LOVE PENCHER

EVOLVING BEAUTY®
EVOLVINGBEAUTY.INFO

*"Of Course
You Can"*

FOUNDER & CEO

PENCHANT

TANYA GALLAGHER

Has a **PENCHANT FOR LOVE**. A love for life, for people and for beauty products that create solutions. "I want my legacy to be one of love, where everyone I encounter comes away feeling loved and valued." Tanya asserts. This enthusiasm transcends to her brand, PENCHANT, an amazing ingrown hair serum. This type of affection is integrated into every brand touch point; from product order to product experience—stellar!

My morning routine is.....

I'm a super early riser; I love getting a jump start on the day. I wake up to a glass of warm lemon water. Then, I'm off to the gym by 5 AM for either a run or some weight training. Those good endorphins give me the best feeling that really carries throughout the day! Then I shower, grab a healthy breakfast, and get started checking in with work. Early morning hours are super productive for me.

I started my own business because.......

I wanted to solve a problem and open the doors of conversation. I also wanted to have a job that satisfies the many aspects of my personality - the creative side and the business side. Being the boss, you wear a lot of hats. The role gives you a chance to enact change at every level of your organization and call all the shots. If it doesn't work, it's on you, but when things work out, it's incredibly rewarding to know that your ideas have come to life.

Penchant provides luxe problem-solving skin products, including our signature ingrown hair serum, Penchant Bare. It's like a miracle-worker fighting against red bumps and ingrown hairs!

The best advice I ever received is....

To listen to your intuition. Every time I've made a gut decision in either my business or my personal life it's yielded the best results. Going along with that, I totally believe in good vibrations, and that good energy attracts more good energy. Having a positive mindset is key, which is why I start my day doing things that make me happy and why I focus on the good things even in challenging circumstances.

How has the Digital Age changed your business? Highs/Lows...

I wouldn't have the business I have today without E-Commerce and Social Media. Penchant first launched products to the Amazon platform and it gave the business an active, engaged market. At the same time, there's always new competition out there, so staying true to your brand is key.

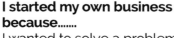

I AM
CREATIVE
+ INTIUITIVE
ACTION ORIENTED

PENCHANT

Tanya is originally from Philadelphia, PA. She graduated from UCLA with a degree in Communications. She currently resides in Seattle, Washington.

MONTH:

MY PERSONAL STATEMENT FOR THE YEAR

"Find Your Tribe."-PT

SUNDAY	MONDAY	TUESDAY	WEDNESDAY	THURSDAY	FRIDAY	SATURDAY

GRATITUDES/NOTES

Visualize the completion of your Personal, Professional and Physical goals.
*Your monthly goals should align with your **Brand Mastery Priorities** from Step 1.*

My Personal Intention is...
1
2
3

My Professional Intention is...
1
2
3

My Physical Intention is...
1
2
3

DATE:

THIS WEEK'S GOAL

EVOLVING
BEAUTY

THE PLANNER
ESSENTIAL TACTICS TO BEING
happy
&
SUCCESSFUL

THIS WEEK'S PRIORITIES	MONDAY	TUESDAY	WEDNESDAY
	TODAY'S GOAL	TODAY'S GOAL	TODAY'S GOAL
	PRIORITIES	PRIORITIES	PRIORITIES
	1	1	1
	2	2	2
	3	3	3
	4am	4am	4am
	5am	5am	5am
	6am	6am	6am
	7am	7am	7am
	8am	8am	8am
	9am	9am	9am
	10am	10am	10am
	11am	11am	11am
	12am	12am	12am
	1pm	1pm	1pm
	2pm	2pm	2pm
	3pm	3pm	3pm
	4pm	4pm	4pm
	5pm	5pm	5pm
	6pm	6pm	6pm
	7pm	7pm	7pm
	9pm	9pm	9pm
	10pm	10pm	10pm

ERRANDS

POSITIVE PATTERNS

	S	M	T	W	T	F	S
PHYSICAL							
PERSONAL							
PROFESSIONAL							

THE PLANNER
ESSENTIAL TACTICS TO BEING
happy
& SUCCESSFUL

THURSDAY		FRIDAY		SATURDAY		SUNDAY	
TODAY'S GOAL		TODAY'S GOAL		TODAY'S GOAL		TODAY'S GOAL	
PRIORITIES		**PRIORITIES**		**PRIORITIES**		**PRIORITIES**	
1		1		1		1	
2		2		2		2	
3		3		3		3	
4am		4am		4am		4am	
5am		5am		5am		5am	
6am		6am		6am		6am	
7am		7am		7am		7am	
8am		8am		8am		8am	
9am		9am		9am		9am	
10am		10am		10am		10am	
11am		11am		11am		11am	
12am		12am		12am		12am	
1pm		1pm		1pm		1pm	
2pm		2pm		2pm		2pm	
3pm		3pm		3pm		3pm	
4pm		4pm		4pm		4pm	
5pm		5pm		5pm		5pm	
6pm		6pm		6pm		6pm	
7pm		7pm		7pm		7pm	
9pm		9pm		9pm		9pm	
10pm		10pm		10pm		10pm	

DISTRACTIONS THIS WEEK	BIG IDEAS THIS WEEK

DATE:

EVOLVING BEAUTY

THE PLANNER
ESSENTIAL TACTICS TO BEING
happy
& SUCCESSFUL

THIS WEEK'S PRIORITIES	MONDAY	TUESDAY	WEDNESDAY
	TODAY'S GOAL	TODAY'S GOAL	TODAY'S GOAL
	PRIORITIES	PRIORITIES	PRIORITIES
	1	1	1
	2	2	2
	3	3	3
	4am	4am	4am
	5am	5am	5am
	6am	6am	6am
	7am	7am	7am
	8am	8am	8am
	9am	9am	9am
	10am	10am	10am
	11am	11am	11am
	12am	12am	12am
	1pm	1pm	1pm
	2pm	2pm	2pm
	3pm	3pm	3pm
	4pm	4pm	4pm
	5pm	5pm	5pm
	6pm	6pm	6pm
	7pm	7pm	7pm
	9pm	9pm	9pm
	10pm	10pm	10pm

ERRANDS

POSITIVE PATTERNS

	S	M	T	W	T	F	S
PHYSICAL							
PERSONAL							
PROFESSIONAL							

THE PLANNER
ESSENTIAL TACTICS TO BEING
happy
& SUCCESSFUL

THURSDAY		FRIDAY		SATURDAY		SUNDAY	
TODAY'S GOAL		TODAY'S GOAL		TODAY'S GOAL		TODAY'S GOAL	
PRIORITIES		PRIORITIES		PRIORITIES		PRIORITIES	
1		1		1		1	
2		2		2		2	
3		3		3		3	
4am		4am		4am		4am	
5am		5am		5am		5am	
6am		6am		6am		6am	
7am		7am		7am		7am	
8am		8am		8am		8am	
9am		9am		9am		9am	
10am		10am		10am		10am	
11am		11am		11am		11am	
12am		12am		12am		12am	
1pm		1pm		1pm		1pm	
2pm		2pm		2pm		2pm	
3pm		3pm		3pm		3pm	
4pm		4pm		4pm		4pm	
5pm		5pm		5pm		5pm	
6pm		6pm		6pm		6pm	
7pm		7pm		7pm		7pm	
9pm		9pm		9pm		9pm	
10pm		10pm		10pm		10pm	

DISTRACTIONS THIS WEEK	BIG IDEAS THIS WEEK

DATE:

THIS WEEK'S GOAL

EVOLVING BEAUTY
THE PLANNER
ESSENTIAL TACTICS TO BEING
happy
& SUCCESSFUL

THIS WEEK'S PRIORITIES

MONDAY	TUESDAY	WEDNESDAY
TODAY'S GOAL	TODAY'S GOAL	TODAY'S GOAL

PRIORITIES	PRIORITIES	PRIORITIES
1	1	1
2	2	2
3	3	3
4am	4am	4am
5am	5am	5am
6am	6am	6am
7am	7am	7am
8am	8am	8am
9am	9am	9am
10am	10am	10am
11am	11am	11am
12am	12am	12am
1pm	1pm	1pm
2pm	2pm	2pm
3pm	3pm	3pm
4pm	4pm	4pm
5pm	5pm	5pm
6pm	6pm	6pm
7pm	7pm	7pm
9pm	9pm	9pm
10pm	10pm	10pm

ERRANDS

POSITIVE PATTERNS

	S	M	T	W	T	F	S
PHYSICAL							
PERSONAL							
PROFESSIONAL							

THURSDAY		FRIDAY		SATURDAY		SUNDAY	
TODAY'S GOAL		TODAY'S GOAL		TODAY'S GOAL		TODAY'S GOAL	
PRIORITIES		PRIORITIES		PRIORITIES		PRIORITIES	
1		1		1		1	
2		2		2		2	
3		3		3		3	
4am		4am		4am		4am	
5am		5am		5am		5am	
6am		6am		6am		6am	
7am		7am		7am		7am	
8am		8am		8am		8am	
9am		9am		9am		9am	
10am		10am		10am		10am	
11am		11am		11am		11am	
12am		12am		12am		12am	
1pm		1pm		1pm		1pm	
2pm		2pm		2pm		2pm	
3pm		3pm		3pm		3pm	
4pm		4pm		4pm		4pm	
5pm		5pm		5pm		5pm	
6pm		6pm		6pm		6pm	
7pm		7pm		7pm		7pm	
9pm		9pm		9pm		9pm	
10pm		10pm		10pm		10pm	

DISTRACTIONS THIS WEEK	BIG IDEAS THIS WEEK

DATE:

THIS WEEK'S GOAL

THIS WEEK'S PRIORITIES	MONDAY	TUESDAY	WEDNESDAY
	TODAY'S GOAL	TODAY'S GOAL	TODAY'S GOAL

	PRIORITIES	PRIORITIES	PRIORITIES
	1	1	1
	2	2	2
	3	3	3
	4am	4am	4am
	5am	5am	5am
	6am	6am	6am
	7am	7am	7am
	8am	8am	8am
	9am	9am	9am
	10am	10am	10am
	11am	11am	11am
	12am	12am	12am
	1pm	1pm	1pm
	2pm	2pm	2pm
	3pm	3pm	3pm
	4pm	4pm	4pm
	5pm	5pm	5pm
	6pm	6pm	6pm
	7pm	7pm	7pm
	9pm	9pm	9pm
	10pm	10pm	10pm

ERRANDS

POSITIVE PATTERNS		S	M	T	W	T	F	S
PHYSICAL								
PERSONAL								
PROFESSIONAL								

THE PLANNER
ESSENTIAL TACTICS TO BEING
happy & SUCCESSFUL

THURSDAY		FRIDAY		SATURDAY		SUNDAY	
TODAY'S GOAL		TODAY'S GOAL		TODAY'S GOAL		TODAY'S GOAL	
PRIORITIES		PRIORITIES		PRIORITIES		PRIORITIES	
1		1		1		1	
2		2		2		2	
3		3		3		3	
4am		4am		4am		4am	
5am		5am		5am		5am	
6am		6am		6am		6am	
7am		7am		7am		7am	
8am		8am		8am		8am	
9am		9am		9am		9am	
10am		10am		10am		10am	
11am		11am		11am		11am	
12am		12am		12am		12am	
1pm		1pm		1pm		1pm	
2pm		2pm		2pm		2pm	
3pm		3pm		3pm		3pm	
4pm		4pm		4pm		4pm	
5pm		5pm		5pm		5pm	
6pm		6pm		6pm		6pm	
7pm		7pm		7pm		7pm	
9pm		9pm		9pm		9pm	
10pm		10pm		10pm		10pm	

DISTRACTIONS THIS WEEK	BIG IDEAS THIS WEEK

DATE:

THIS WEEK'S GOAL

EVOLVING BEAUTY

THE PLANNER
ESSENTIAL TACTICS TO BEING
happy
& SUCCESSFUL

THIS WEEK'S PRIORITIES	MONDAY	TUESDAY	WEDNESDAY
	TODAY'S GOAL	TODAY'S GOAL	TODAY'S GOAL

	PRIORITIES		PRIORITIES		PRIORITIES	
	1		1		1	
	2		2		2	
	3		3		3	
	4am		4am		4am	
	5am		5am		5am	
	6am		6am		6am	
	7am		7am		7am	
	8am		8am		8am	
	9am		9am		9am	
	10am		10am		10am	
	11am		11am		11am	
	12am		12am		12am	
	1pm		1pm		1pm	
	2pm		2pm		2pm	
	3pm		3pm		3pm	
	4pm		4pm		4pm	
	5pm		5pm		5pm	
	6pm		6pm		6pm	
	7pm		7pm		7pm	
	9pm		9pm		9pm	
	10pm		10pm		10pm	

ERRANDS

POSITIVE PATTERNS

	S	M	T	W	T	F	S
PHYSICAL							
PERSONAL							
PROFESSIONAL							

THE PLANNER

ESSENTIAL TACTICS TO BEING

happy
& SUCCESSFUL

THURSDAY		FRIDAY		SATURDAY		SUNDAY	
TODAY'S GOAL		TODAY'S GOAL		TODAY'S GOAL		TODAY'S GOAL	
PRIORITIES		PRIORITIES		PRIORITIES		PRIORITIES	
1		1		1		1	
2		2		2		2	
3		3		3		3	
4am		4am		4am		4am	
5am		5am		5am		5am	
6am		6am		6am		6am	
7am		7am		7am		7am	
8am		8am		8am		8am	
9am		9am		9am		9am	
10am		10am		10am		10am	
11am		11am		11am		11am	
12am		12am		12am		12am	
1pm		1pm		1pm		1pm	
2pm		2pm		2pm		2pm	
3pm		3pm		3pm		3pm	
4pm		4pm		4pm		4pm	
5pm		5pm		5pm		5pm	
6pm		6pm		6pm		6pm	
7pm		7pm		7pm		7pm	
9pm		9pm		9pm		9pm	
10pm		10pm		10pm		10pm	

DISTRACTIONS THIS WEEK	BIG IDEAS THIS WEEK

MONTHLY REFLECTION

Visualize, in gratitude, Achieving Your Goals
Use the senses to see, hear, smell,
and touch the experience of what your success will look and feel like.

	MONTHLY GOAL		ACHIEVEMENT
1			
2			
3			

	PERSONAL	TIME SPENT	TACTICS FOR IMPROVEMENT
1			
2			
3			
	PROFESSIONAL		
1			
2			
3			
	PHYSICAL		
1			
2			
3			

1. WHAT DID I LEARN THIS MONTH?
1.
2.
3.
4.
5.

2. DISTRACTIONS AVOID / FEARS TO FORGE THROUGH
1.
2.
3.
4.
5.

3. PEOPLE I LEARNED FROM OR INSPIRED ME?
1.
2.
3.
4.
5.

4. MISSED OPPORTUNITIES THIS MONTH?
1.
2.
3.
4.
5.

5. WHAT ACTIONS CAN I CORRECT FOR NEXT MONTH?
1.
2.
3.
4.
5.

HOW DID I SPENT MY TIME THIS MONTH?
*KEEP BRAND MASTERY PRIORITIES &
PERSONAL STATEMENT TOP OF MIND.
WHAT YOU SAY AND DO SHOULD ALIGN.

PERSONAL
___% Time

PROFESSIONAL
___% Time

PHYSICAL
___% Time

192

NOTES

NOTES

SHEENA WILDER
THE BRAND VOICE

"Be Bold &
Truthful in
Everything You Do
and You'll Achieve
the Desired
Outcome"

FOUNDER & CEO

SHEENA WILDER

Has always been a great communicator. Getting her point across is a part of her DNA. It makes sense that she'd create a firm that speaks as the **THE BRAND VOICE** for clients. Sheena launched PR Primas in 2001, in-part, to prove to herself that African American women can be successful in public relations. Today, PR Primas is the go-to company in the public relations landscape.

"Never compromise who you are to secure a client."

PR Primas is a beauty and lifestyle-centric public relations firm. Marketing, brand enhancement, crisis management, social media and event execution is the firm's focus.

I AM A **BOLD** *HONEST* **ACHIEVER**

If I could tell my younger self something about being an entrepreneur... Find an amazing mentor and soak up all the knowledge. Even with a mentor, you have to decipher what will work for you. What works for one person, may not be the case for you. I have two great mentors. David Morris, he gives me the best business advice. My Mom gives me the best life advice.

My morning routine is...
I'm up every morning at 5:30 am. I check emails, text messages and social media first. Next, I wake my son and get him ready, and take him to school. I return home and begin my day within an hour.
TIP: Make a daily to-do-list for organization, to remember important tasks and not feel overwhelmed.

On Work/Life Balance...
I struggle with this daily but, it's getting better. As an entrepreneur, you are always working. Schedule days for your spouse, family, and friends.

The Digital Age, Highs/Lows?
The good is that you have the opportunity to reach thousands of people from every demographic with a click of a button. The bad is it is not personable; I miss the relationships and in-person talks.

My business is distinct because...
My point of difference is focused on building memorable brands. I like to take on clients that have something different to offer or have a niche that hasn't quite been tapped into. My methods are untraditional and very creative.

Sheena was born and raised in Atlanta, GA where she lives with her family. She holds a Mass Communication degree from the University of Florida. For more information go to PRPrimas.com | @PRPrimasInc

EVOLVING BEAUTY

THE PLANNER
ESSENTIAL TACTICS TO BEING
happy
& SUCCESSFUL

MY PERSONAL STATEMENT FOR THE YEAR

MONTH:

"When we give cheerfully and accept gratefully, everyone is blessed. --Maya Angelo

SUNDAY	MONDAY	TUESDAY	WEDNESDAY	THURSDAY	FRIDAY	SATURDAY

Visualize the completion of your Personal, Professional and Physical goals.
*Your monthly goals should align with your **Brand Mastery Priorities** from Step 1.*

My Personal Intention is...	1
	2
	3
My Professional Intention is...	1
	2
	3
My Physical Intention is...	1
	2
	3

GRATITUDES/NOTES

DATE:

EVOLVING
BEAUTY

THE PLANNER
ESSENTIAL TACTICS TO BEING
happy
& SUCCESSFUL

THIS WEEK'S PRIORITIES

MONDAY	TUESDAY	WEDNESDAY
TODAY'S GOAL	TODAY'S GOAL	TODAY'S GOAL

PRIORITIES	PRIORITIES	PRIORITIES
1	1	1
2	2	2
3	3	3
4am	4am	4am
5am	5am	5am
6am	6am	6am
7am	7am	7am
8am	8am	8am
9am	9am	9am
10am	10am	10am
11am	11am	11am
12am	12am	12am
1pm	1pm	1pm
2pm	2pm	2pm
3pm	3pm	3pm
4pm	4pm	4pm
5pm	5pm	5pm
6pm	6pm	6pm
7pm	7pm	7pm
9pm	9pm	9pm
10pm	10pm	10pm

ERRANDS

POSITIVE PATTERNS

	S	M	T	W	T	F	S
PHYSICAL							
PERSONAL							
PROFESSIONAL							

THE PLANNER
ESSENTIAL TACTICS TO BEING
happy
& SUCCESSFUL

THURSDAY		FRIDAY		SATURDAY		SUNDAY	
TODAY'S GOAL		TODAY'S GOAL		TODAY'S GOAL		TODAY'S GOAL	
PRIORITIES		PRIORITIES		PRIORITIES		PRIORITIES	
1		1		1		1	
2		2		2		2	
3		3		3		3	
4am		4am		4am		4am	
5am		5am		5am		5am	
6am		6am		6am		6am	
7am		7am		7am		7am	
8am		8am		8am		8am	
9am		9am		9am		9am	
10am		10am		10am		10am	
11am		11am		11am		11am	
12am		12am		12am		12am	
1pm		1pm		1pm		1pm	
2pm		2pm		2pm		2pm	
3pm		3pm		3pm		3pm	
4pm		4pm		4pm		4pm	
5pm		5pm		5pm		5pm	
6pm		6pm		6pm		6pm	
7pm		7pm		7pm		7pm	
9pm		9pm		9pm		9pm	
10pm		10pm		10pm		10pm	

DISTRACTIONS THIS WEEK	BIG IDEAS THIS WEEK

DATE:

THIS WEEK'S PRIORITIES

MONDAY	TUESDAY	WEDNESDAY
TODAY'S GOAL	TODAY'S GOAL	TODAY'S GOAL

PRIORITIES		PRIORITIES		PRIORITIES	
1		1		1	
2		2		2	
3		3		3	
4am		4am		4am	
5am		5am		5am	
6am		6am		6am	
7am		7am		7am	
8am		8am		8am	
9am		9am		9am	
10am		10am		10am	
11am		11am		11am	
12am		12am		12am	
1pm		1pm		1pm	
2pm		2pm		2pm	
3pm		3pm		3pm	
4pm		4pm		4pm	
5pm		5pm		5pm	
6pm		6pm		6pm	
7pm		7pm		7pm	
9pm		9pm		9pm	
10pm		10pm		10pm	

ERRANDS

POSITIVE PATTERNS

	S	M	T	W	T	F	S
PHYSICAL							
PERSONAL							
PROFESSIONAL							

THE PLANNER

ESSENTIAL TACTICS TO BEING

happy
&
SUCCESSFUL

THURSDAY		FRIDAY		SATURDAY		SUNDAY	
TODAY'S GOAL		TODAY'S GOAL		TODAY'S GOAL		TODAY'S GOAL	
PRIORITIES		PRIORITIES		PRIORITIES		PRIORITIES	
1		1		1		1	
2		2		2		2	
3		3		3		3	
4am		4am		4am		4am	
5am		5am		5am		5am	
6am		6am		6am		6am	
7am		7am		7am		7am	
8am		8am		8am		8am	
9am		9am		9am		9am	
10am		10am		10am		10am	
11am		11am		11am		11am	
12am		12am		12am		12am	
1pm		1pm		1pm		1pm	
2pm		2pm		2pm		2pm	
3pm		3pm		3pm		3pm	
4pm		4pm		4pm		4pm	
5pm		5pm		5pm		5pm	
6pm		6pm		6pm		6pm	
7pm		7pm		7pm		7pm	
9pm		9pm		9pm		9pm	
10pm		10pm		10pm		10pm	

DISTRACTIONS THIS WEEK	BIG IDEAS THIS WEEK

DATE:

THIS WEEK'S GOAL

THE PLANNER
ESSENTIAL TACTICS TO BEING
happy
& SUCCESSFUL

THIS WEEK'S PRIORITIES	MONDAY	TUESDAY	WEDNESDAY
	TODAY'S GOAL	TODAY'S GOAL	TODAY'S GOAL
	PRIORITIES	PRIORITIES	PRIORITIES
	1	1	1
	2	2	2
	3	3	3
	4am	4am	4am
	5am	5am	5am
	6am	6am	6am
	7am	7am	7am
	8am	8am	8am
	9am	9am	9am
	10am	10am	10am
	11am	11am	11am
	12am	12am	12am
	1pm	1pm	1pm
	2pm	2pm	2pm
	3pm	3pm	3pm
	4pm	4pm	4pm
	5pm	5pm	5pm
	6pm	6pm	6pm
	7pm	7pm	7pm
	9pm	9pm	9pm
	10pm	10pm	10pm

ERRANDS

POSITIVE PATTERNS

	S	M	T	W	T	F	S
PHYSICAL							
PERSONAL							
PROFESSIONAL							

THE PLANNER
ESSENTIAL TACTICS TO BEING
happy
& SUCCESSFUL

THURSDAY		FRIDAY		SATURDAY		SUNDAY	
TODAY'S GOAL		TODAY'S GOAL		TODAY'S GOAL		TODAY'S GOAL	
PRIORITIES		PRIORITIES		PRIORITIES		PRIORITIES	
1		1		1		1	
2		2		2		2	
3		3		3		3	
4am		4am		4am		4am	
5am		5am		5am		5am	
6am		6am		6am		6am	
7am		7am		7am		7am	
8am		8am		8am		8am	
9am		9am		9am		9am	
10am		10am		10am		10am	
11am		11am		11am		11am	
12am		12am		12am		12am	
1pm		1pm		1pm		1pm	
2pm		2pm		2pm		2pm	
3pm		3pm		3pm		3pm	
4pm		4pm		4pm		4pm	
5pm		5pm		5pm		5pm	
6pm		6pm		6pm		6pm	
7pm		7pm		7pm		7pm	
9pm		9pm		9pm		9pm	
10pm		10pm		10pm		10pm	

DISTRACTIONS THIS WEEK	BIG IDEAS THIS WEEK

DATE:

THIS WEEK'S GOAL

THIS WEEK'S PRIORITIES	MONDAY	TUESDAY	WEDNESDAY
	TODAY'S GOAL	TODAY'S GOAL	TODAY'S GOAL
	PRIORITIES	PRIORITIES	PRIORITIES
	1	1	1
	2	2	2
	3	3	3
	4am	4am	4am
	5am	5am	5am
	6am	6am	6am
	7am	7am	7am
	8am	8am	8am
	9am	9am	9am
	10am	10am	10am
	11am	11am	11am
	12am	12am	12am
	1pm	1pm	1pm
	2pm	2pm	2pm
	3pm	3pm	3pm
	4pm	4pm	4pm
	5pm	5pm	5pm
	6pm	6pm	6pm
	7pm	7pm	7pm
	9pm	9pm	9pm
	10pm	10pm	10pm

ERRANDS

POSITIVE PATTERNS		S	M	T	W	T	F	S
PHYSICAL								
PERSONAL								
PROFESSIONAL								

THE PLANNER
ESSENTIAL TACTICS TO BEING
happy
& SUCCESSFUL

THURSDAY		FRIDAY		SATURDAY		SUNDAY	
TODAY'S GOAL		TODAY'S GOAL		TODAY'S GOAL		TODAY'S GOAL	
PRIORITIES		PRIORITIES		PRIORITIES		PRIORITIES	
1		1		1		1	
2		2		2		2	
3		3		3		3	
4am		4am		4am		4am	
5am		5am		5am		5am	
6am		6am		6am		6am	
7am		7am		7am		7am	
8am		8am		8am		8am	
9am		9am		9am		9am	
10am		10am		10am		10am	
11am		11am		11am		11am	
12am		12am		12am		12am	
1pm		1pm		1pm		1pm	
2pm		2pm		2pm		2pm	
3pm		3pm		3pm		3pm	
4pm		4pm		4pm		4pm	
5pm		5pm		5pm		5pm	
6pm		6pm		6pm		6pm	
7pm		7pm		7pm		7pm	
9pm		9pm		9pm		9pm	
10pm		10pm		10pm		10pm	

DISTRACTIONS THIS WEEK	BIG IDEAS THIS WEEK

DATE:

THIS WEEK'S GOAL

EVOLVING BEAUTY

THE PLANNER
ESSENTIAL TACTICS TO BEING
happy
& SUCCESSFUL

THIS WEEK'S PRIORITIES	MONDAY	TUESDAY	WEDNESDAY
	TODAY'S GOAL	TODAY'S GOAL	TODAY'S GOAL

	PRIORITIES	PRIORITIES	PRIORITIES
	1	1	1
	2	2	2
	3	3	3
	4am	4am	4am
	5am	5am	5am
	6am	6am	6am
	7am	7am	7am
	8am	8am	8am
	9am	9am	9am
	10am	10am	10am
	11am	11am	11am
	12am	12am	12am
	1pm	1pm	1pm
	2pm	2pm	2pm
	3pm	3pm	3pm
	4pm	4pm	4pm
	5pm	5pm	5pm
	6pm	6pm	6pm
	7pm	7pm	7pm
	9pm	9pm	9pm
	10pm	10pm	10pm

ERRANDS

POSITIVE PATTERNS

	S	M	T	W	T	F	S
PHYSICAL							
PERSONAL							
PROFESSIONAL							

THE PLANNER
ESSENTIAL TACTICS TO BEING
happy
& SUCCESSFUL

THURSDAY		FRIDAY		SATURDAY		SUNDAY	
TODAY'S GOAL		TODAY'S GOAL		TODAY'S GOAL		TODAY'S GOAL	
PRIORITIES		PRIORITIES		PRIORITIES		PRIORITIES	
1		1		1		1	
2		2		2		2	
3		3		3		3	
4am		4am		4am		4am	
5am		5am		5am		5am	
6am		6am		6am		6am	
7am		7am		7am		7am	
8am		8am		8am		8am	
9am		9am		9am		9am	
10am		10am		10am		10am	
11am		11am		11am		11am	
12am		12am		12am		12am	
1pm		1pm		1pm		1pm	
2pm		2pm		2pm		2pm	
3pm		3pm		3pm		3pm	
4pm		4pm		4pm		4pm	
5pm		5pm		5pm		5pm	
6pm		6pm		6pm		6pm	
7pm		7pm		7pm		7pm	
9pm		9pm		9pm		9pm	
10pm		10pm		10pm		10pm	

DISTRACTIONS THIS WEEK	BIG IDEAS THIS WEEK

MONTHLY REFLECTION

Visualize, in gratitude, Achieving Your Goals
Use the senses to see, hear, smell,
and touch the experience of what your success will look and feel like.

	MONTHLY GOAL	ACHIEVEMENT
1		
2		
3		

PERSONAL	TIME SPENT	TACTICS FOR IMPROVEMENT
1		
2		
3		
PROFESSIONAL		
1		
2		
3		
PHYSICAL		
1		
2		
3		

1. WHAT DID I LEARN THIS MONTH?
1.
2.
3.
4.
5.

2. DISTRACTIONS AVOID / FEARS TO FORGE THROUGH
1.
2.
3.
4.
5.

3. PEOPLE I LEARNED FROM OR INSPIRED ME?
1.
2.
3.
4.
5.

4. MISSED OPPORTUNITIES THIS MONTH?
1.
2.
3.
4.
5.

5. WHAT ACTIONS CAN I CORRECT FOR NEXT MONTH?
1.
2.
3.
4.
5.

HOW DID I SPENT MY TIME THIS MONTH?
* KEEP BRAND MASTERY PRIORITIES &
PERSONAL STATEMENT TOP OF MIND.
WHAT YOU SAY AND DO SHOULD ALIGN.

PERSONAL
___% Time

PROFESSIONAL
___% Time

PHYSICAL
___% Time

NOTES

Photo by @Jerrina Montgomery | Hair by Barry Reynolds | @BarryLifestyles | MakeUp by @theGlammatory

ABOUT THE AUTHOR

PHYLENCIA "PT" TAYLOR is a Consultant, Culturalist, Adjunct Educator, and Philanthropist. She's the founder of EVOLVING BEAUTY® Brands, powered by Shine Beauty Culture, A Boutique Brand Management & Research Consultancy, established in 2007.

A native of Buffalo, NY, Phylencia has worked with C-Suite Executives at Fortune 500 companies such as Wella Corporation, Carol's Daughter, Johnson Products and Sean Combs Enterprises. She is passionate about creating tools for women to boost their evolution. Her debut book, Evolving Beauty, The Business of Beauty in a New Age was released in 2016. As a Culturalist, she studies how beauty, image, and identity shape the world around women.

Taylor has an affinity for research, big data and marketing/communication strategies. A MA from American University and BBA from Clark Atlanta University. Founder of Shine Magazine, (defunct) For Beauty Professionals and Enthusiasts and former Editorial Director of Dollar General's Beauty Cents Magazine. When she isn't consulting, you can find her on TV-One's "For My Man," as a recurring Culturalist or speaking on business, women, beauty or image-centric topics.

She lives in a suburb of Atlanta, Ga with her son.

EVOLVINGBEAUTY.INFO

CPSIA information can be obtained at www.ICGtesting.com
Printed in the USA
LVIW01n1537181017
552886LV00011B/123

* 9 7 8 1 5 4 2 8 2 4 9 1 0 *